Rennell Rodd

Feda

With other Poems, Chiefly Lyrical

Rennell Rodd

Feda
With other Poems, Chiefly Lyrical

ISBN/EAN: 9783744776431

Printed in Europe, USA, Canada, Australia, Japan

Cover: Foto ©Thomas Meinert / pixelio.de

More available books at **www.hansebooks.com**

FEDA

WITH OTHER POEMS, CHIEFLY LYRICAL

BY

RENNELL RODD

AUTHOR OF "POEMS IN MANY LANDS, ETC

WITH AN ETCHING BY HARPER PENNINGTON

London

DAVID STOTT, 370, OXFORD STREET, W.

MDCCCLXXXVI.

A VOLUME of poems needs no preface, but nevertheless I take this opportunity of recording my gratitude for the appreciation which my former volume met with at the hands of my critics two years ago.

Of the present series, the longest, Féda, was written in great part, some time ago, and is, doubtless, full of the faults of youth. It seemed to me, however, that the attempt to treat a simple story of modern life from the poetic side, contained sufficient of novelty to justify its publication. For the other poems, I ought to feel satisfied, if they prove to any one that the privilege of dwelling with beauty, the understanding of Nature's moods and the desire to look beyond, are not wholly inconsistent with the "storm and whirl" of active life.

Finally, I trust, I may be forgiven for having attempted to cast a softer light upon the dark old legend of the "Wandering Jew," which still prevails so strongly among the superstitious of some parts of Europe.

R. R.

BRITISH EMBASSY, BERLIN.
Nov. 1885.

CONTENTS.

	PAGE
FEDA: A Story	5
LYRICS—	
The Journey Home	104
Albano	110
Reverie: An Italian Night	112
Night-Voices	118
Prague	120
The Skylarks	125
Richard Wagner	128
Victor Hugo	130
The Nature Child	134
I knew a Poet	140
Lyrics—I. "The form in which her spirit moved"	142
II. "Though I be half of common clay"	142
III. "Two Flowers in a world's garden"	143
In Winter	144
Spring's Pardon	145
The pity of it	146
To ——	147
Song	148
Good-bye. To a Child	150
A Memory	151
A Nocturne of Chopin	153
At Worst	155
At Best	162
"Whether in Dawn's grey gold"	165
Credo	167
THE HERMIT'S TALE	185
PETRARCH: A Monologue	201
THE END OF THE QUARREL	212
JUBA'S DEATH	214
A PICTURE	218
A DEDICATION	219

FEDA:
A Story.

*Und wann ist Lieb am reichsten?—
Das ist sie wenn sie giebt,—
Und, Spricht, wie redet Liebe?
Sie redet nicht,—sie liebt!*
                              HALM.

FEDA: A STORY.

I.

Far on the sea-washed border of fair France,
In Southern sunlands, where the fire-flies dance
Through long spring nights till June goes after May,
Between the waters and the hills there lay
A town of cool paved streets and shaded ways,
A pleasant refuge in scorched autumn days,
Girded with gardens, where what warm winds blew
Were sweet with roses all long summer through.

The old walls crumble down, no sentry waits
To cry his challenge in her open gates,—
Her towers have seen no gleam of armoured men
Since Martel drave the flying Saracen;—
But ferns droop down from many clefts and rents,
Long grasses wave in all her battlements,

And only children laughing at their play
Keep siege and battle in the old gate-way.

Yet few things change, the grey walls moulder on,
The hills give back the cloister carillon;
The goat-bells ring from ridge to rocky ridge,
And through the valley by the wattled bridge
In slow procession up the mountain path
The reapers bring their evening aftermath.

One half the crescent of its red-rocked bay
Sloped gently down from where a convent lay,
With many a shrine, among dark olive trees,
And pathway winding to the parted seas.
There oft at eve the fisher-folk would climb,
When suns were setting, and the Ave-chime
Rang welcome home, to where the cypress waves
Above a sleeping sisterhood of graves,
And watch their shadows lengthen out and fall
Across that wonder of the cloister wall,
Where some old Tuscan who had strayed so far
Had drawn their Saint of little Castellar.

Such quiet cares the white-robed sisters had
Who lived forgotten of the world, and glad,—
To trim the lamps before their Lady's feet,
And keep the flowers in her chalice sweet,
Or bind her wreath with gentle willing hands.

And some came thither out of far off lands,
To lose the world a little while, and stayed
And laid their sorrows in that cypress shade;
And some came there to bury deep their dead;
And some to whom life was a book unread,
That in the after-world their lips might kiss
The Master's feet without one taint of this.

The peace of God was on their lives,—no day
Brought any tiding from the world's highway;
Far out to sea they watched the great ships pass;
The first spring violet in the cloister grass
Was such a thing to them, the first lark's song,
Who lived with fisher folk the whole year long.

There came one thither on the tide of time,
Half-child half-woman, when the spring's young prime

Was starriest with narcissus, ere those vales
Grew mad with music of the nightingales,—
Came there, and lingered, till a golden moon
Grew full-orbed in the singing skies of June,
And fire-flies dimmed their lustre in the tree:
Till all the peasant-folk would watch to see
A slight white figure pass, who seemed to wear
The whole sun's glory in her golden hair,
The sea's deep colour in her wide blue eyes,
And loved the greeting of her soft replies,
And all the troubled beauty of her face.

For she had come to that enchanted place
With a child's first great sorrow, having known
One life to love that twined about her own
Far north in their Loire valley,—and he was dead,
And she, with strangers all uncomforted,
Stayed in that convent on the Southern shore.

She had the features of one gone before,
He had said, the kind grave man who seldom smiled,
But only loved her, loved her: and the child
Heard in a reverend wonder;—far apart

In the green vineyard country, heart in heart,
They two had lived together all her days;
His love had been her faith, and his least praise
Her earthly gladness; the world's storm and strife
Had come not near the whiteness of her life.
There he, half dreamer half philosopher,
Had bared the treasure of his soul to her,—
Bestowed on all her wonder-time of youth
Whate'er on earth is consecrate to truth,
Through holy thoughts of great lives dead and gone
To heights of hope still waiting to be won,—
Those harvests gathered from the thousand years
In love unrecompensed, in untold tears
By hero teachers of the hero time,
And hero singers of the world's grey prime.

But as days gathered, and the young child grew,
She learned the secret of his heart, and knew
The shadow of a lost gladness darkening still
That wore the little thread of life, until
His thoughts would drift farther and far away,
His eyes would wander strangely,—so one day

They called a frightened child to his bedside,
And he just smiled, and smiling on her died.

   Then they had brought her southward; she was grown
Almost a woman, very fair, alone
In a dark shadow that she knew not of,
With those dead years, and nature and her love.
And she had no one in the world—save here
The mother's sister—simple and severe,
The abbess,—one indeed who meant her well,
Only she hoped Féda would learn to dwell
Contented here, when the young dreams were flown,
And never miss a life she had not known.
She little guessed how strange a dwelling place
Had genius chosen in that young child's face
And flowerlike frail form, what wild unrest
Of wonder-dreams, what longings unrepressed
Burned in her, whispered by that voice which stirs
The quick heart-beat of God's own choristers.

   Wayward and loveable,—she would not heed
Those books the white-robed sisters bade her read.

She only said—"I pray you bear with me,
"Who was not taught to see as others see;"
Would answer low, with lips put up to kiss,
"Because it was my father taught me this.
"I know he would not tell me wrong," she said,
"It is so little while since he is dead,—
"And you will leave me free a little yet,
"To dream my dreams, and wander, and forget."

So first they did not reason with her mood,
And left her free to wander where she would,
Having no fear because of her sweet face,
Among the quiet dwellers of that place.

And all those woods were hers to wander through,
From summer-dawning to the even-dew;
Those hills, where still the orange-gardens told
The old-world fable of the fruit of gold,
And all the loveliness of earth was there:
Such flowers to bind in garlands for her hair,
Such skies to wonder at, such songs to sing,
Such changeful dreams for her imagining.

And so it was Féda was grown to be
Known to all dwellers by that summer sea ;
Perchance the shadow of the convent cast
A kind of reverence round her : where she passed
Not one would dare to follow, lest he scare
That gentle presence. And since she came there
Men whispered there had been no blight to spoil
The orange-blossom, but the golden oil
Swelled larger berries on their olive trees,
And stormy nights broke never near those seas.

Only at times the labourer on the hill
In the orange groves when noon lay very still
With drowsy scent of blossom, pausing, heard
A sound that was no song of any bird,
No reed of shepherd piping to his flocks,
A voice that rang through the wave-hollowed rocks
Fresh, ever-changing, rising—falling,
To hear the echo answer back its calling,—
And crossed himself at those sweet carollings,
And told his fellow, " the white lady sings.'

For she would sit and make song after song
In some far olive wood the whole noon long,

Striving to answer in her song the speech
Of birds and waters, if she too might reach
The hidden heart of nature—learn to know
The charm revealed through music long ago
To that old singer of the dawn of days,
Who made such melody in mountain ways
That down the shadowy hollows, stealing, came
The frightened woodland things with eyes aflame,
And listened ever and grew less afraid,
Till on his knees the white doe laid her head,
And stared out sorrow from her brimming eyes;
The lark dropped silent from the songless skies,
And pressed a throbbing bosom on his feet;
The lizard lying in the noonday heat
Looked up to wonder; the loud stream grew still,
And brought no story from the silent hill;
No least wave fretted on the glassy seas,
And all the branches of the windless trees
Were set with little heaving throats of birds,
That sat and wondered why the song had words.

 So in her singing she forgot her care,
Till that midsummer noon when Adrien found her
 there.

II.

He who should sail at earliest dawn of day,
Thence steering ever eastward and away,
Would make at sunset in the even-rose
A land that lies under the Alpine snows,
Of pine-woods leaning to a townless shore,
With mountain ridges rising o'er and o'er
Deep creek and islet, where the tideless sea
Breaks white about the shores of Italy—
And dropping anchor at their feet, behold
The sweeps of hill-slope burning into gold,
Afar the forests mystically blue,
Rocks flaming upwards with the sunset hue,
Dark cleft and gully deepening into caves,
And the day dying in the wine-red waves.

In such a little arm of rock encurled,
A still untravelled corner of the world,
Set round with many a trellised vine and flower,
Stands the half-ruin of a fortress tower
Of long-forgotten days. Some old corsair
Perchance had made his little kingdom there—

There like a sea-bird nested on the steep
Had watched his windy empire of the deep,
While down beneath him in the sheltered bay
The crimson dragon of his war-ship lay.

So there were two came once at dawn of day,
From over the dark waters,—watched the mist
Roll upwards, and the mountain peaks cloud-kissed
Break with their forests from the twilight shroud,
And the young sky grow faultless of one cloud;
And they had climbed the rocky rise, and found
The broken castle in its garden ground,
Rich with a wild inheritance of flowers
Forgotten hands had planted round the towers.

And by the door a fisher's net was hung
Where the vine wandered round the porch, and clung
To a worn sword and crescent rudely graven;
And they had called the place the "Quiet Haven."

They hardly knew what years had rolled away,
Nor what they had begotten since the day
When the old lonely dwellers of that place
Came forth and gladdened at a stranger's face:

Since they had stood together hand in hand
That sundown gazing from the extreme land,
Watching the stars grow bright along the shore,
And Adrien said, "We will not wander more."

He was the elder, Adrien—tall and fair,
And strong of limb, with sunny English hair,
Fronting deliberate with such honest eyes,
Eyes soft as woman's, that could ill disguise
The thoughts they flashed with, very deep and kind,
Leaving a sense of sympathy behind
Where'er they lighted :—not in years alone,
A few years, yet far older; he had known
The great refusals, fought and overcome,
Chosen the better part, and now his home
Was all the wide world; he had dared and passed
Through storm and failure, and stood free at last.

His was the self-less spirit; while on earth
The shadow falls that curses in the birth,
While one lies pillowed in eternal ease
With heavy eyelids, so he hardly sees
The children's hunger and the brave man's need,
And mother hearts that labour on and bleed,

Perchance that he may lay a loveless head
On ever softer pillows:—while men dare to say
God wills the world so, and not we who pray
He may but keep us in the easy way;
While yet is twilight over lands that weep,—
The weak keep silence and the strong men sleep;
While man and man on earth dwell side by side,
With the great gulf between them fixed—more wide
Than sundering mountains, or the sea that parts,
That old inheritance of alien hearts:—
While something whispers in the ear, "Be true,
We shall not always be so lost, so few:"
On earth will be such restless spirits still,
Fools, dreamers, poets, heroes—what you will!

They come at times with fearless voice and high
To look the mad world in the face, and cry
Out on its mock ideals, and to part
The veil and drive one arrow to the heart,
To strip the spectre of his robe and crown;—
Then what a storm of tongues will hoot them down,
And cry blasphemer, being well content
To reason their God's ways were never meant

To take too much in earnest.—Well, what then,
If God be with them, and we be but men!

So it had fared with Adrien, for his hands
Were sacrilegious; he, the lord of lands,
Had set the dangerous precedent, resigned
His birthright; he was one who undermined
Old institutions, smiled at social needs;
Godless no doubt,—none such have any creeds!—
A poet if you will, but then how sad
To write so sanely and to be so mad!

Mad! Well, then welcome madness, for God's sake
Let's rave together! If he strove to take
The whole world's burthen in his arms to bear,
The whole world's sorrow in his heart to wear,
It was a splendid madness,—a high dream.

But he had drunk of that eternal stream,
That whoso tasteth thirsts through all his years,
Because its waters are so salt with tears;

The stream whose course is through the whole wide
    earth,
And mirrored therein are the death and birth
Of Beauty and Joy and Sorrow, and things to be
Lie where its waters mingle with the sea.
He saw one truth in all the world, above
Codes and philosophies, that Law of Love,
To whose control God slowly moves the world.
No life on earth that has it not impearled—
It may be under ocean weeds, and deep,
Lost in the hollow where the tide-drifts sleep,
Or stifled in the turbid whirl of storm,
Yet living surely, gathering to inform
The souls it dwells in. And he knew the price
Of Love on earth is weighed in sacrifice.

  Therefore he broke his prison's gilded bars,
And into night not bright with many stars,
Like a caged bird set free, his spirit flew,—
The cage-born bird that flits the deep wood through,
From tree to tree from cottage eaves to eaves,
And fears the freedom of the forest leaves,

And flies and flies and dare not furl its wing,—
So is it alway unto those who sing.

  Thus, half mistrusting freedom, he had grown
A wanderer over many lands, had known
The ways of many peoples,—he had found
Much love in lonely dwellings, by the sound
Of melancholy Northern seas, in lands
Of man forgotten, and on Southern sands
In Arab tents, and in the village homes
More favoured, he was known as one who roams,
Who comes and goes, and ever leaves behind
Some good remembered.

                His was the rare mind
That grasps the general, lives its life outside
Of use and accident, and stares dream-eyed
On calmer outlines in a statue-land,
That holds blind Faith for ever by one hand,
Sees hardly, only strains towards the light,
Because man's wrong can never be God's right!

  Oh, the large heart of youth! He had assailed
Too boldly, madly, and those half-means failed;

Now the wild flame of youth's desire was spent,
That willed things unattainable; content
To do the thing he knew within his reach,
Not strain for any star in heaven, to teach
The faith of truth, touch hearts to love, and souls
With soft reproof, to aim at lowlier goals,
Yet work as surely in the same high quest,
With human means, and let God heed the rest.

   He, wandering once with Anton—with the friend
Who would have followed to the world's far end
For Adrien's sake—by chance had fared that way,
And found the little tower at dawn of day,
Cut off from all the world, and they had made
Their dwelling here, unknown and unbetrayed.
Our hearts are fettered by the hands we love;
There seemed no better way to pass above
Desire, than after many years of strife,
To build this little wall about their life;
Here, hand in hand through peaceful fall of days,
Here, in the far-off world-forgotten ways,
Self-centred only in their work to tell
The secret that the angel whispers well.

The younger Anton was half Southern born,
A painter's son, the child of many tears
Left in a lonely world too soon—long years
Since Adrien found him with a breaking heart,
A boy and friendless, severed from the art
That was his nature, and had seen and known
The dawning power, and made that love his own;
They had been more than brothers, friends that knew
The other's heart was wholly tried and true.

It had gone well with Anton since they met;
The road had been so smooth, and no regret
Of that past youth had ever made less loud
The ring of his gay laughter, left a cloud
Across the southern beauty of his face.

At times he wandered from their dwelling-place,
And went awhile into the world, but soon
He wearied, and came back before the moon
Had waned, whose rising called him forth;
It seemed so grey, he said, in their cold North.

Fame had not failed him, but it did not mar
His restless effort, for he felt how far

The summer skies are from the lark's desire,
What heights were still to conquer, and the fire
Burned upward ever, and men's praise or blame
Had moved him little; it was not for fame
He laboured, but for Art's sake, heeding not
How far the rest remembered or forgot.

Yet there was something wanting—he was made
Of strange, conflicting elements; men said
His art was cold, too calmly perfected
And passionless, and hard to understand.
He, too, had dwelt in Adrien's statue-land;
And it was all ideal, far removed
From daily life of men that lived and loved,
Half strength, half-weakness, only shadowing truth;
He needed some strong purpose in his youth,
To gather many wandering aims; too long
He waited upon Adrien's word, not strong
To trust his own heart's prompting; life and art
Had failed to find communion, and apart
It lacked the " natural touch ";—maybe his hour
Was not yet come, only the dawning power
Was there in Anton;—then a form and face

Like some young god come down to run the race
With the lithe athletes, far away out-borne
Beyond their reach to laugh his laugh of scorn,
And pass his way, inconstant as the foam,
Except to Adrien and their haven home.

So here they dwelt outside the world and free,
Even as one who fares in the wide sea,
But steers for ever by the extreme land
So near that he may almost reach his hand,
And snatch a bud of the overhanging rose,
Or hear the children laughing, and he knows
The gladness of the earth, and heeds no more
The cares and passions of the peopled shore.

III.

There was a village on a jutting crest
Of olive-gardened mountain, a sea-nest
Of mouldering walls that fenced one climbing street.
Only poor fisher-folk, whose little fleet

Sparkled at sundawn over all those seas,
Reaping the harvest of the calm ; and these
Were all their neighbours, and in all his life
Old silent Nanno and his shrill-tongued wife
Had fared no further from the ruined tower.

His joy was just to sit hour after hour,
And watch while Anton painted, till at last
Annita's voice came like a thunderblast,
Waking the echoes, ever and again
Enlarging on the idleness of men.
Worthy Annita, you had done her wrong
To judge her by the temper of her tongue ;
A scolding, honest soul, although she held
Mankind in little honour, and compelled
Submission ; he was grown too deaf to feel
The piercing eloquence of each appeal
To this or that Beata,—for she showed
In this her preference of her sex, bestowed
On each their separate functions in her prayers,
Invoked the lesser saints for household cares,
Made this one patron of her shrill surprise,—
Called that to weight her anger,—in her creed

Not one male saint intruded, though indeed
The padre had some reverence, but he too
Was just a man, and like them all, she knew.

There were two pictures in the vaulted hall
Of Anton's half completed, broad and tall,
A year's full labour, in the hero mood
Of the dead mighty masters; long renewed
Unceasing effort;—and therein was told
The story of that after-world of old,
Of singers dreamed who dimly understood
The night of evil and the light of good.

The first, a vision of the Blessed Isles;—
The ripples break in everlasting smiles
On seas more azure than the skies above
Warmed by the summer of the land of love;
Deep banks of flowers broaden to the bays,
The groves are green through pleasant length of days
For gentle presences for ever young;
And highest songs of poets here unsung
Fall with a sweeter cadence, and fair dreams
Of kindred spirits mix like mountain streams

That flow in long communion to the sea,
And deepen into knowledge, silently;
And loyal eyes meet eyes, and hands
Grasp hands, and voiceless each one understands.
And all that wrought in patient love on earth,
And all who held their lives of little worth,
And all that suffered, and the long oppressed
Lie gladly in those meadow lawns at rest.

And then the other—the pale world of hell,—
Grey rustled there the knee-deep asphodel,
O'er dreary waste lands bounded by a mist,
And flitting things that wander where they list,
Like dead leaves fluttered on a lifeless breeze,
Glide hither, thither, through the yellow trees.

There in the midst, almost a child, she stood
Young-eyed as one that died in maidenhood,
The sad pale queen, sad to be young in vain,
And pale for wasted pity and dead pain.
And round her feet and near and far away
Phantasmal forms of lives that lived their day,
And died to all save consciousness of death

Who tasted Lethe with their dying breath,
And lost the souls they knew not ;—for between
The nearer rocks and this folk and their queen
That slow-streamed river wound.

     But near at hand
Were gaunt grey rocks, and wastes of barren sand,
The hither shore, where those whose sin was great
Wail by the margin in the doom of fate ;
They may not traverse that forgetting rill,
But in death's midway must remember still.

 These forms were dimly shadowed, and so much
Was still to do, in each the little touch
That makes or mars perfection, wanted yet.

 All round the grey old castle walls were set
With Anton's studies, and in the midst the clay
Fresh from the master's moulding of to-day,
The Psyche, faith-redeemed and winged and free
And loving, into immortality.

 And Adrien praised, and Anton was content,
So through the vine-porch arm in arm they went

One eve of summer; all the sky was red
With promise of fair weather, and Anton said:—
"To-morrow is the day of Rosalie,
"And I shall go over the hills to see
"Their feast of roses in the little town;
"The moon will be at full to light us down,
"Come with me, you will find, I think, a song
"Among the mountain faces, and too long
"You stay among your books; we shall not miss
"Just one day in Portello, spent like this."
But Adrien said, "I have a mind to sail,
"Or drift or row me, if the wind should fail,
"A few days journey by the coast; this June
"Grows stifling under roof, and now the moon
"Is at the full; so be there wind, how light
"I care not, I will sail somewhere to-night."

It chanced, with sunset rose a gentle breeze,
Rustling the pine-tops and the citron-trees,
And Adrien went below into the bay,
And set the sail, pushed out and fared away,
Where the wind listed under shadowy heights
Transfigured in the moon of Southern nights,

Westward and westward, and the freshening wind
Was life and joy; and soon he left behind
Familiar shapes of mountains,—in his wake
Pales the long moon-path, and the crisp waves break
In frost of silver on his bows, and far
Faint shore-bells seem to ring the music of the Star.

IV.

Now it fell out about the morrow's noon
The wind had died away, and skies of June
Grew pale with intense sunlight,—dreamily
He drifted o'er the intervening sea
Till the clear shallows rippled round his oar,
Cast anchor there, and waded to the shore.
Seeing above how ancient olives made
Deep-columned avenues of mid-day shade;
And thus bare-kneed in his rough seaman's guise,
From ledge to ledge, he scaled the rocky rise,
Till in that twilight of the trees he stood
And heard low music coming through the wood.

He heard and followed where the guiding sound
Strayed o'er the stillness, up a rising ground,
By steep and ferny hollows, till he came
To where among the daisies such a flame
Of starry-leaved anemones burned red,
Such golden shafts from sunbeams overhead
Struck down the shadow,—and saw her sitting there,
A girl's white figure, very young and fair,
Singing the burden of a song he knew,
And wondered what so sweet a child might do,
Alone and singing in a stranger-land.
And then he saw a book was in her hand
Whose songs she made her low sad music of,
And so broke in upon her pause : " What love
" Of thine own kind, what ignorance of pain ! "—
She had been lost in singing, only then
She turned and saw and crimsoned at his smile,
And all was silence for a little while
As each one wondered, only in some far tree
A loud thrush gladdened, and below the sea
In measured cadence lapped the shifting sand,
The bruisèd thyme she held in one small hand
Made all the noon-tide odorous, the glen

Was dark with emerald twilight, now and then,
Like a winged blue-bell flitting through the grass,
A tiny violet butterfly would pass
And dwell from flower to flower in a kiss.

   What strange young presence in the glen was this,
Borne from what far seas hither?   And her eyes
Went up to his, full of a shy surprise:
" And do you know my burden?"—" Ay," he said,
" Though not till now were words and music wed;
" But pardon that I break your quiet so,
" My boat lies anchored in the bay below—
" I thought, perchance, to find some house this way,
" For I have sailed all night since yesterday
" At sundown;—but too strangely here we meet,
" Two aliens in an alien land, to greet
" And pass as quickly!"
                      And she said, " Nay sir,
" But welcome if you be some wanderer!"
—And from her basket in the olive-root
Brought out her white-bread and her store of fruit,
And set them down before him on the grass;—
" For we are bounden to all folk who pass

" By the old cloister-custom,—and, indeed,
" The town is far off, and I have no need."

Now sits he there beside her, who so long
Had heard no voice of woman, save the song
Of some loud-laughing peasant-maid, come down
For Anton's model from the hill-side town,
And he is listening to each simple word
Intent and still—as though he never heard
Such voice of wisdom. She, so glad to teach
The country's story in her father's speech,
Talks on and on, and in a little while
Each heart went to the other, smile to smile,
And eyes to eyes made answer,—each one learned
The other's story, till a red sun burned
Among the gnarlèd trunks, and skies grew gold,
While yet they stayed together, while she told
Of her old home, and how she came to be
Here in the convent by the Southern sea.

" My home was set far in the pleasant ways,
" Where summer lingers and late autumn stays

" Till all the grapes are red on all the hills,
" Where the long valleys ripple down in rills
" To a wide river slowly wending west ;
" And here and there along a grey rock-crest,
" About whose feet some clustered village clings,
" Are antique palaces of great dead kings ;
" Turret and gable and high oriel traced
" With sculptured flower-work, and half effaced
" Strange imagery above the carven door,
" With drawbridge down for ever and evermore ;
" Then far, far inland, over hill and plain,
" Is all green vineyard country of Touraine.
" Westward, beyond that city of dismal fame,
" Where once across the quiet hillside came
" Carrier, the murderers' hireling—came and slew
" The fair young promise of the land, and threw
" Dead men and dying and living side by side
" Into the bleeding river at flood-tide,—
" The sad, grey town that wears those memories still,
" A road winds by the water, skirts the hill
" Above the silvering aspens on the marge,
" So you may see the deep, hay-laden barge
" Drift down the noons of summer in a dream :

" And soon a way leads inland from the stream,
" With poplar-trees in melancholy line;
" Just by the corner is a rock-hewn shrine
" Where Mary mother in her faded wreath
" Looks sadly at a written rhyme beneath :

> ' *Si l'amour de Marie*
>   *Dans ton cœur est gravé,*
>   *En passant pas n'oublie,*
>   *De lui dire un Ave.*'

" I see it always, how the road runs straight
" Up to the yew that shadowed o'er our gate;
" And then beyond the shadow of the yew
" Two walls shut in an orchard avenue,
" A long sweet grass-grown way—where in the spring
" The walls are pink with fruit-trees blossoming,
" A long straight way, and always as you pass
" You scent the violets hiding in the grass :—
" And then the bridge that arches o'er the moat,
" Where such gold leaves of water-lilies float;
" And last, beyond a wilderness of flowers,
" You see the gables and the three grey towers,

" With windows peeping through thick ivy leaves,
" And moss grown golden on the slated eaves,
" And all my swallows had their houses there;
" One pointed turret was a winding stair—
" Almost a little castle, guarded round
" With that deep moat—and in the garden ground
" Were all the simple flowers that to me
" Seem ever sweetest, growing wild and free:
" Dark crimson dahlias and blushing stocks,
" And sunflowers and groves of hollyhocks,
" And trellised walks with roses overgrown,
" And all those beds of flowers were my own—
" It was the sweetest garden ever seen,
" But all would seem so changed now."

       She had been
Lost in the telling, and then sudden grew
Conscious he listened and looked up and knew
And clenched the little rosy fingers fast,
And dared not meet his eyes, and so downcast
Said, " But I weary you."
      Then swift up-springing,
For far away the even bell was ringing,—

"It is the Angelus, I must not stay,
"By now they wonder why I am away.
"Farewell, good stranger, since you do not tell
"The name they call you by."
                          "Yet not farewell,"
He answered, "Let me find you here once more,
"Since we are strangers on this Southern shore,
"Too strangely met to part again so soon."
And so he bound her to the second noon;
"And I may keep the book in which you read,
"To hold you to your pledge?"
                          "Keep it," she said,
"If you would read it, only reason not
"That what I promise is so soon forgot.
"Farewell, and when we meet you too must tell
"The story of your life,—farewell."
                          "Farewell."

She had the walk of some wild wood-born thing,
Erect and free, and ever she would sing
Upon her way; and long time Adrien stood
And watched her figure fading down the wood;

Then first he felt for many a day gone by
A sense of loneliness, and wondered why.

But in the book he read her father's name ;
A name well-known once till a cloud of shame
Had darkened o'er its promise ; all grew clear,
The story he had wondered so to hear,
Their lonely lives together—all that she
Had never known,—and it was so—for he
Had made a life's atonement in her love,
And so forgotten had passed out above
Man's pardon or dispraise ;—all this was so,
But the hard world would never care to know.

Is there a sin in all the world so wide
Love might not veil it o'er and wholly hide,
As all its dead are hidden in the seas ?
God knows the earth is full of lives like these,
And many a heart grows white again within,
Washed of its one deep staining and the sin
Which men forgive not and which God forgave ;
Peace upon earth ! But even in the grave

The dead men sleep not, o'er our ways are cast
Such sunless shadows darkling from their past.

Then he went seaward, and he pondered long,—
Ah me, he thought, and in a while her song
Will fade, and leave her little life forlorn,
No hand to shield her from the breath of scorn,
To ward between her and the world's hard ways
And keep the secret buried all her days.
And ever in his heart such pity grew
For this frail child and the strange tale he knew.

And still the sunset flared across the sea,
But the warm air was windless, lifelessly
His painted sail was drooping from the mast,
The oar's plash broke the silence as he passed
That tiny haven, and in tears of gold
The water from his lifting oar-blades rolled;
Day's end was fair as ever poet dreamed
In orient worlds of summer, and there seemed
A strange new beauty touching common things,
A presence in the air of unseen wings

Sailing from yonder sunset, wafting near
Through the enchanted silence in his ear
A promise of things dimly seen,—and far
Over the rose-flush rose the best loved star.

   Then night fell suddenly, not far away
The village lights were mirrored in its bay,
And down the still air fell the convent chimes,
Completing that strange concord which at times
Attunes our mood to Nature's mood, and brings
Mystic fraternity twixt souls and things.
He saw the line of towers dimly traced
In shadow-land, as by enchantment placed
Between two skies, the mirrored and the true,
And, nearing, marked the cypress avenue
Closing the cloister stations, and a light
Over the fast-closed gate, "Sleep, child, sleep well.
    good-night."

V.

The after-morrow he sailed back that way,
And left his boat at anchor in the bay
Till darkness gathered with the even dew;
And so on many morrows, till he knew
She would not fail at noontide when he came.

And he had learned to call her by her name,
Baptised Félicitá, and short, Félise,
Or Féda, as her baby lips would please
His love, who taught them lisping. She was born
At Florence, in that quarter, on the morn
Of St. Felicitas, the saint who gave
Her seven sons into one fiery grave
For the faith's sake, and followed, giving praise
That she had seen them nobly end their days
In the old time of struggle. Therefore she
Was called Félicitá; and it should be
A happy omen for the child, they said.

And in the Lily city, too, was laid
The life that died for her to live; since then
They never went to that first home again,
But it was ever to him as a shrine
That held the memory of some divine
Past presence, where he dared not walk alone.

" And yet," she said, " I seem to know each stone
" In Giotto's tower, and every winding street,
" And every name in Florence sounds as sweet
" As music and as home. And, oh! to see
" Just once my city,—only once to be
" In San Miniato's graveyard, looking down
" Across the stream, the bridges, and the town,
" Over the roofs and gardens, right away
" To the far Carrara mountains,—some blue day,
" I might be almost happy—so it seems—
" If they be happy that fulfil their dreams."

Oh! those were goodly days when each one learned
To know the other, till his whole soul yearned
To lift the shadow from that young child's heart;
And many a noon they met again, to part

With " till to-morrow," in the even dim :
And needed that to-morrow; then with him
That unknown sense of loneliness first grew,
Nor passed when many gathered, and he knew
For him was now but one face fair of all
Fair faces, one voice seeming musical,
One only in whose presence was content.

And so the sunny June days came and went.

She was an endless wonder; most he loved
The whiteness of her heart, so far removed
Above the world's mistrust, that she could bring
Her books to read with him, or sit and sing—
Those bursts of song the mountain echoes stole—
In perfect open innocence of soul :
The world had never touched her, pure as truth
And trusting all, and unashamed of youth.

So wise in years, so innocently young—
When he would chance upon her as she sung,
He seemed to see around her, sitting there,

Mute angels, listening for some new sweet air
To sing in the high heavenly place.
       Then oft
She told him of their life, with voice grown soft
Almost to weeping, and grave eyes bent low :
It was so lonely there ; " How should they know
" Or feel what I feel, who but come and go
" Between blank wastes of nunnery wall, soul-bound
" From morn to eve, in one eternal round
" Of prayers and aves, and so wholly miss
" The essence and the end of prayer in this
" The symbol, and they think to make me stay
" In this pale sisterhood for ever and a day.

"Oh, my good friend, I think I have such faith
" As his was, such as trusts in love, and saith,
" ' Be glad to live, nor care to question why ;'
" We cannot reason out that mystery—
" We only know that ever, day by day,
" Old wrongs and shadows slowly wane away,
" That naught recurs as it has been before,
" But always better ; that the light is more,

" And human lives win slowly through the gloom,
" From that sad sentence of eternal doom
" To hope of fair things far away ;—for me
" Are endless wonders, that they cannot see
" Walled in their narrow bounds; when overhead
" The morning sun streams in upon my bed :
" It is the sun that wakes me, not the stain
" Of the Saint's passion pictured on the pane,
" But in their cells the very window-bars
" Are set so close they never see the stars ;
" And I am weary when they only say,
" ' Child, if thine heart is troubled, kneel and pray.' "

Then there came round the festa-morn whereon
Their patron saint was honoured ; she was gone
Home to her convent, and for three long days
He would not see her,—so he went his ways
Among the villages and up the brow
Of the sea-mountains. He was quite sure now
That he had found out love ;—her wistful face
And all her ways, and every maiden grace
Of speech or gesture had become a part
Of his own life, and there was in his heart

A strange unrest of gladness ; a great light
Had broken in upon his days, more bright
Than he had known or dreamed of, and the world
Put on new glories, and the dawns unfurled
A lordlier pageantry, and everywhere
Seemed waves of joy that thrilled through the quick air
Intense and real, and the fields and trees
Had a near meaning, and far o'er the seas
He smiled to watch the little sails go by,
Sun-gold between the water and the sky,
And sang, "sail on, your seas are not so wide,
" But love has havens on the farther side."

Then once he saw her, for the convent town
Was decked with flowers, and the nuns came down
In long procession, and the streets were gay
With banners, the sea-folk kept holiday—
And all the boats along the shore were dressed
With flags or branches, and the grey priest blessed
Their nets and tackle and the fishing gear,
As was the custom there since many a year.

He saw one figure, as he watched unseen,
Bearing a wreath of woven evergreen,
A white rose here and there,—she rather seemed
Some old-world daughter such as Anton dreamed,
Bound for a rustic altar in the wood
Of Faunus or Pomona, as she stood
Leading the music with that voice of hers,
Among the incense-bearing choristers.
Then they swept onward, and the chanting died
Among the echoes on the farther side,
And she was gone.
     How long the hours seem
When love is waiting; and how like a dream
That flits to waking ere we hold it fast,
They hurry when love enters in at last!
So, slowly, slowly the long days went by
Till once again their trysting time was nigh.

Yet morning waxed to noontide, and the noon
Waned slow and sultry, and the living tune
Of song-birds silenced in the midday glow;
He heard the chiming hours come and go
Across the drowsy silence, long, so long

From chime to chime; and then again the song
Of some loud wood-bird rang reveille out clear,
Till every tree was singing far and near.
And still she tarried, and he reasoned not—
For love is humble, and she hath forgot,
He thought, maybe that the three days are past,
But she will come to-morrow; then at last
In the long shadows that the even cast,
He saw her white dress flutter through the trees.

And now a red sun kissed the margin of the seas.

VI.

And they are sitting in the olden place,
Under the gnarlèd olive tree; her face
Is even graver than its wont, her eyes
Are wet and wistful, and the fierce thoughts rise
As Adrien listened to the tale she told

" For we shall never meet here as of old,
She said; " I wonder shall we any more

" But I must live my days out on this shore,
" Through many a weary year. It must be so,
" For I have nowhere in the world to go,
" Being a woman and so young, dear friend
" I knew that soon these better days would end,
" And if a little sooner, well, the loss
" Is mine. Someday, somewhere, our ways may cross,
" When I am free, who knows? and I shall spring
" To greet you, and, may be, you'll bid me sing
" The songs of the old, pleasant noons we spent.

" It was his birthday; the first day I went,
" And we were used to be so merry then,
" In the old home up North, and therefore when
" His day came round, the first he was not by—
" I had no heart to tell the abbess why—
" Only I wanted to be all alone,
" And keep my day of memories for my own.
" And on that morn the abbess bade me stay,
" Too long already I had had my way,
" And Sister Agnes waited me to read;
" And then I answered that I had no need
" For Sister Agnes; that his books I brought

" Were all I cared to read in; that I thought
" I wanted none to read with me; and then
" The tears came when I thought on him again.

" But this it was that angered her, she said
" Better was prayer than weeping for my dead—
" Since sorrow brings no loved one back again—
" That God might sooner ease him of the pain
" They doom their dead to—I should feel it best
" To bring him nearer to the perfect rest.

" And then I answered, but if God were good,
" I knew there were no pains for him who stood
" Above their blame or censure. Oh, my friend,
" I see no hope for any prayer to mend
" The earthly sorrow; when our hearts are set
" In throbbing blood, to bid us not regret!
" There was one voice on earth, to us was sweet :
" What shall atone for silence,—shall we meet
" Among the myriads in the unknown land ?
" We miss the pressure of a parted hand—
" Shall that console us, can we quite forego
" The only life we yet have learned to know,

" Resign so wholly the near need of love
" For stranger glories that we know not of?
" And do they think, if any love or prayer
" Could bring me nearer, I should leave him there?

" But she was angered, meaning to be kind,
" She said I had strange fancies in my mind,
" And wild rebellious instincts ; it were best
" These wayward impulses should be repressed ;
" And so she bade me lay my whole soul bare
" At next confession, when the priest comes there.
" And they have taken all his books away,
" As full of dangerous doctrines ; and they say
" I may not wander as I used to do,
" Alone, among the mountains.   Is it true
" That any here could harm me ?   Oh ! my friend,
" Our pleasant readings in the wood must end,
" And it were idle to rebel in vain.

" So I was patient, that just once again
" I might steal out alone, and find you here,
" And tell you from my heart how very dear

" These days were, when we read his books and
    talked
" Of the great lives who made them, when we walked
" The perfect way of that enchanted land
" That is where two souls meet and understand.
" Now all is over, over ;—I must turn
" Back to the melancholy life, and learn
" To wait in patience and forbear, for so
" He would have had me always, and I know
" There is no other way ; and now, farewell.
" But thank you ever, as no word can tell ;
" And you must think of me sometimes, when far,
" As of a bird that beats against the bar,
" And knows that in the world outside is spring,
" And wants to fly into the clouds and sing."

Then she was rising silently, and this
Was all his answer, with her hand in his
He stayed her rising, and she saw him kneel
Beside her and above, and she could feel
His breath upon her hair, his arm that curled
About her, as to shield her from the world,
His soul surrounding and upholding her :

In all the woods there was no faintest stir ;
And then the long-restrained, strong manhood broke
Into the fire and eloquence of love ; he spoke
Of hope renewed, and promise and release,
And golden days of gladness, and great peace,
Of fair fulfilment of all high desires
In God's great gift, the love that never tires ;
Of sweet forgetting after many tears,
And long accord of kindred hearts, the years,
Young years to love in,—till his very soul
Rushed through his lips, unfettered of control,
And trembled into whispering—" Will you come ? "

And all the while she listened scared and dumb.

At last she rose erect before him there,
And nerved as one whose lips appeal to prayer
To speak out truth, so in despite of dread
She looked into his eyes and calmly said :
" Yes, I will go with you and be your wife,
" And learn what I have longed for all my life ;
" I say not that I love, I have not known—
" I that have lived my quiet life alone—

"What love may mean, but only I am glad
"When I am with you,—I that was so sad.

And she put out her little hand to his,
So their lips grew together in one kiss ;
He wondered then how all his days were spent
Ere love made known his crowning sacrament.
Then hand in hand as lovers use they went,
Glad and half-fearful through the darkening wood,
Till by the free waves on the shore they stood.
He lifted her in his strong arms to bear
Her arms about his neck, and all her hair
Falling about his forehead, and her breast
That beat and trembled on his heart at rest ;
While round and round late seagulls whirled and flew,—
This was the fairest eve that ever Adrien knew.

It is late even, all the hills are dim,
And she has gone over the sea with him ;
The light wind blew, the little bark sped fast,
The wide waves roll between her and the past.

VII.

And it was living joy for her to be
Sailing to freedom on that moonlit sea;
And close she clung to him, and could not speak:
Almost he dared to think across her cheek
Blushed the aurora of the dawn of love,
And, never doubting how the end might prove,
Felt such a royal happiness within
That dazed him with excess of joy, to win
At last one thing worth winning, by whose side
What chance might come would all be glorified;
To hold her fast whose every heart-beat thrilled
Like warm blood to his own—life's life fulfilled
In strong, pure, passionate, splendid love, the crown
To which all other hopes and ends bow down,
Because this end is selfless, and above
Mistrust or failure, this that says, "I love."

And the light sea-wind kissed her eyes to rest,
Laid like a child to slumber on his breast.

She was his own for ever, and a throb
Of joy possessed him, nothing now could rob
His life of triumph,—and he watched her there,
So sweetly young, so innocently fair,
How could she know love's mystic meaning yet!
He was so sure of gladness he could wait.

On! till the moon grew pale as a wan mist,
And the stars faded; then he bent and kissed
Gently the golden hair upon her brow,
And so she woke, and wondering: "Tell me now,
" How far we sail and whither! Oh, I see
" The morn is breaking, tell me, where are we?"

And then he pointed to the lightening East;
" I have a friend in Genoa, a young priest,—
" This is our wedding-morning. He and I
" Faced death together in the fields up North,
" In the old student days—when we went forth
" A crowd of boys with such a heart of fire,
" Knowing the time was come, the long desire
" Waited and wept for, when from sea to sea,
" From Alp to Alp, should Italy be free.

"There is so much that I have yet to tell,—
"These will be tales for winter evenings;—well,
"I fought there too, whose word is alway peace.
"Who labour to the time when wars shall cease,
"And nations learn a nobler law than fear.

"Yet there are burthens that no man may bear:
"I speak not now of kingdoms and their pride,
"And all the blood that falls unjustified,—
"No, not of lands and passions—but the price
"Of freedom must be paid in sacrifice,—
"And unto each his country and his cause
"Is where men suffer, where unequal laws,
"Not self-imposed, breed misery and keep down
"The natural heart-beat, and an alien crown
"Is one mere jewel that a stranger wears,
"And purple robes are dyed with blood and tears.

"How eagerly we mustered then, mere boys,
"Whose gentle ears had never heard the noise
"Of cannon-thunder, boys whose lives were sweet
"With all Hope's promise—how they burned to meet
"The hireling armies, in the Lombard plain,

" And fought not vainly, if it be not vain
" To win for each his natural birthright here ;
" To rid the land of alien lords, and clear
" The air of threats and stifled sobs, so he
" Unslaved and unashamed may breathe it free.
" He was struck down there in the field they call
" From Solferino, the last field of all.
" Those days of madness, it was then we knew
" The war was over, and the eagle flew
" Back to his nest beyond the barrier snows.

" How that day ended ! the fierce sun that rose
" On battle, waned in storm and sank in calm,
" And the cool fell on weariness, the balm
" Of twilight, the still stars came one by one
" To wonder, and the moon looked down upon
" Pale faces staring upward with blank eyes ;
" That summer night was broken with such cries
" As shudder through the memory still ; and he
" Lay wounded there under the stars with me
" Unscathed through all the battles.—Ah ! how long
" That night was, till the misty dawn grew strong
" Over the eastward mountains, and again

" The sun burned down on all that human pain
" We saw such things about us, child, not well
" For you to listen to or me to tell.
" And yet above the corpses and the blood
" The lark uprose as ever, with its flood
" Of throbbing welcome to the rising sun,
" And the old mountains smiled on battles won
" In calm sad silence,—Then we seemed to feel
" God's presence on the dawn ; he tried to kneel,
" And fell back fainting, and lay like one dead :—
" He had been the wildest of us all who led
" The student life together, but from then
" His world was changed, and when we met again
" The Church had claimed him,—once in jest I said :
" He should be priest if ever I was wed."

And while he spoke the sun had lifted o'er
The silver gleaming waters, and the shore
Grew nearer with its dotted towns, and soon
Their boat was left at anchor,—long ere noon,
With merry jangling of the horses' bells,
They rushed through seashore villages, by dells
Of age-old olive wood, above the bays,

White fringed and sapphire, up steep winding ways
Hewn in the rock side, here and there a town
Of fisher-folk, unburdened of renown,—
Grey-walled and slumbrous,—little worlds may be
With lives lived out in silence by the sea,
Only the gulls to witness,—and they passed;
And each new scene seemed fairer than the last:
A strange new glory lighting up the face
Of desolation! Each small sun-kissed place
Seemed set to witness this his joy, and say,
" Oh well with us, for love has passed this way."

And in the city of palaces they two
Bound fast their lives together; though he knew
She was so young still, and that love of his
Was pure and holy as an angel's kiss,
Yet so he willed it, that no taint of shame
Should ever breathe upon her gentle name
To bind her fast and justify their flight,
Not ever doubting she had chosen right.
That night, half fearfully, as one who goes
To some high shrine of reverence, and knows
A holy presence near to him, he crept

Into the young wife chamber ere she slept;
So flower-like she lay, so fair, so young,
So like a veil of innocence were hung
The soft, white curtains of her maiden bed
About the tired eyes and golden head,
She seemed to him to be so pure a thing
Love might but hover near with gentle wing,
And holier sleep breathe low his soft-drawn sighs.
He kissed her open lips, and so her eyes
Went up to his and saw love gazing through,
Then gently closed; and this was all of love she
    knew.

Then there came word to Anton on a day,
Why he had been these many weeks away,
How one was coming in awhile to be
Queen in their little kingdom by the sea,
And Anton's heart misgave him as he read;
"His joy will come between our lives," he said.

VIII.

Then they went Southward slowly,—lingering long,
Through old-world towns whose each name is a song,
Those sweet old towns of story, where they stand
Tower-crowned and silent in their slumber-land;
How rest they now after the stormy years,
How weep at leisure long-owed mother tears!

The fissures widen in these yellow walls
Close-leaning, where no sun-light ever falls,
And the roofs over-lap; only out there
A Campanile bleaches in the glare
Of noon-tide, and the very doves fly down
Into the shaded side. Ah, grey old town,
How tired art thou, how effortless! The weed
Fringes thy paving boulders, and, indeed,
Thou art more ghostly than the ghosts that walk
Thy shadowy porches yonder,—though their talk
Wakes never an echo in the silent street

With the last word from Florence, or how the fleet
Came back to Pisa from the warring East,—
Or what they plan in yonder little nest
Sparkling in sun-floods on the last blue crest,
To fire the youngest of thy hero-brood,
And fret the edges of the ancient feud.

Yet these are phantoms with the streaming hair
Under the grey steel helmet, clustering there,
Ringing the crimson banner, and thine eyes
Dream, for the air is quick with memories.

They will not march through the wide gate again
For any feud or foray, nor shall strain
Of battle-chorus echo down thy dells,
Nor evermore the clang of those loud bells
Proclaim Madonna watching from the wall;
Ah fallen, fallen, yet loveliest in thy fall,
Throned o'er the hills, like a forsaken queen!

Only the mules in yon dark shadow lean,
And a monk mutters somewhat down the street,

Only a sudden rush of children's feet
Vexes thy slumber, or the homeward song
Of labouring folk at eve.

       All August long
They wandered through the cities of romance,
To soft Siena in her ageless trance,
Arezzo citadelled with corn and flowers,
And Santa Fina's mountain crown of towers,
Cortona's, Chiusi's Tuscan graves, and down
The Arno valley to the silent town
Where voices wane to whispers, lest one sound
Should mar the quiet of that burial ground
Where rest her great forgotten. Such a sleep
As theirs is, one might envy, could we keep
That sense of sweet surrounding, laid beneath
In such an Earthly Paradise of death;
The heart of Pisa seems to slumber here
Safe in the frescoed cloister, and in ear
Of faint sea-winds that nod the cypress tree.

There is a time for places—you should see
Rome first at day-dawn, Naples at late noon,
And Venice in the full spring's golden moon,
But Florence first at sunset; so he deemed
Who knew them at all seasons.
     Yet it seemed
The noon was long in Prato to delay,
When Florence was but such a little way,
For all Fra Lippo's frescoes in the dim
Old choir, and Donatello's marble hymn
Of singing children,—ever till the chime
Rang on toward even, asking "Is it time?"
"And is it really Florence," she would say,
"Home to my Florence that we go to-day?"
"And are we really on the road at last?"
While vineyard hills and villages fled past;—
And then the throb of joy to be indeed
In her own city of the lily-mead,
Where still among the palace piles and shrines
And hurry and din of laughter, one divines
The scent of lilies in the evening air,
Hears yet the lute-strings ring across the
 square

Of nobles, to full Tuscan tones that reach
Nearer the heart than any earthly speech.

    The world is sunset's,— one first frightened star
Shows over ancient Fiesoli, and far
As eye may follow down the crimson west,
A golden river winds away to rest
Among the ruby mountains. 'Tis the hour
Of Ave, and each stone in Giotto's Tower
Shows a more perfect jewel,— while the doves
Fly to their roosting, and a voice like Love's
Whispers across the silence ; down the stream
That shaft of flame that is the last day-gleam
Wanes, lingers, dies ; the parting orb that kissed
Yon mountain edges draws a purple mist
Over dark cypress clusters and the wood,
Fringing the silvered marges, red as blood
Those clouds are still that see Him overhead ;
A boat is drifting down the river-bed, —
Again the lute strings and the plaintive air,—

Yonder's the tower of Carmine, and there
San Miniato on the twilight hill.

All this makes Florence: so she had her will.

IX.

At last one autumn evening they were come
Over the hills above their castle home :
Far down beneath the little tower glowed
In sunset, while he led the mule she rode,
And down the path the merry mule-bells rang :
And forth to meet them from the vine porch
    sprang
Anton, elate and eager,—and they met :
A splendid light of manhood, taller yet
Than Adrien, with his reckless Southern eyes
Gladdening with welcome, warming with surprise.
And that rich voice of his broke loud and strong,
With "welcome, sister, I have waited long
"And stayed pursuit,—and here at last you ride

"Into your silent realm at eventide."—
And lightly from her seat she leapt and took
His hand and thanked him with a gentle look,
And Adrien watched his wonder and was proud.

Then up came old Annita, shrilling loud,
With "Blessed Santa Lucia, help my eyes!
"Is it God's angel come down from the skies?
"Or are they all such angels in your land?"
And womanly and quick to understand
She did her gentle service,—while no less
Grey Nanno smiled his willing helplessness.

There then they three took up the quiet life,
And all did homage to the young girl wife,
And watched and waited on her as a child,
Deeming it full repayment if she smiled.
And in the distant village homes her name
Was rumoured as a saint's, and when she came
Young mothers brought their youngest to be
    blessed,

And children crowded round to be caressed,
And the rough seamen whispered soft and low
Lest one forbidden word should overflow,
And there was something added to their days,
The touch of sympathy, the word of praise,
A better influence, a joy, a light;
Then Adrien knew that she had chosen right.

And most of all it gladdened him to see
How Anton learned to care for her, and she
Grew less afraid,—ere long that wistful face
Was grown the Psyche's, and he seemed to trace
Fair forms like hers among the wandering souls,
In Anton's Happy Isles; pale aureoles
Round just such waving hair, and they would
    sing
Together, and by such a little thing
At night if Anton whispered, "Lest she wake,"
He felt, he learns to love her for my sake.

So the days shortened, and long eves fell soon;
Still night by night, under the autumn moon,

They rowed on the calm waters; she would bring
A lute that Anton strung for her, and sing
Song after song when all the world was still,
Only the oars would plash, and hill to hill
Repeat the air in echoes; then it seemed
That life was sweet as ever poet dreamed
In present gladness, with the skies profound,
Star-lovely, over them, and all around
Ripple of water, sea's breath, and sweet sound.

SONG.

A night wind, low and tender,
   Is fretting the silver sedge,
While the moon in a mist of splendour
   Lifts over the mountain edge.

It marks with a soft insistance
   The kiss of the earth and sky,
And reveals in a dream of distance
   The hamlets perched on high.

Do you wonder what they are dreaming
   In the mountain homes up there,

Where the first moonrays are streaming,
And the far-away seems near?

Do you think they muse and wonder
At the distant lands they see,
And say, " In the vales low under
" Are there folk who love like we ? "

X.

And so the autumn passed, and winter grew,
The skies turned grey, and flocks of wild birds flew,
Strange voices through the twilight, overhead ;
Then first there shadowed o'er his heart a dread,
As some small cloud climbs up the noonday blue,
And the sun smiles imperiously through,
But yet the white wings muster, till at last
The whole blue heaven is dark and overcast,—
A doubt, that gathered to an aching fear
That day by day he seemed to be less near
To her, less needed, that surely in her face
The child's look he had loved grew hard to trace,

And graver ever were her earnest eyes,
Less eager questioning for his replies,
That there was something she half seemed to hide.

He could not bear to have her from his side,
And like a faithful hound with his true gaze
He followed where she went, and when the days
Grew shortest, and at night they read together
In the old painted Hall,—when the rough weather
Tumbled the waves among the rocks below,
When the whole bay was one white sheet of snow,
And the wind whistled through the creaking doors,
He thought " It is too lonely on these shores."

He had not marked how suddenly she grew
From child almost to woman, but he knew
How every little gesture, turn of head
Or way the words fell, how each least word said
Was grown a part with his own life, a need,
A bond whence nevermore could he be freed.

It hurt him that she seemed so grateful, asked
His pardon who but needed to be tasked,

For troubling him in aught, that she remained
Child-reverent still, yet all the while constrained :
Something misgave him, for it seemed as though
Love was no nearer than those months ago
When she had answered him, " I do not know
" What love may be, but only I am glad
" When I am with you, I that was so sad."
Something misgave him, he had meant so well,
And darker yet the silent shadow fell.

Then oft he asked her if she ailed in aught,
And gladdened as she looked at him and caught
His smile, and strove to comfort him in vain,
" When the spring comes I will be well again."

Now Anton's winter task was well nigh done,
Both pictures fair and finished, save in one
A group he lingered over, that should be
The master-note, where fettered knee to knee,
The soul of Paris and the faithless bride
Wail by the margin of that dolorous tide
They may not traverse, and ever dimly seen

A wraith like Menelaus frowns between,
And still divides them in the twilight place.

And once again he painted Féda's face,
Because there was no fairer face on earth,
For Helen's,—and half in earnest half in mirth
He drew his own for Paris, but the king
Failed somewhere alway,—with the spring
The pictures must go North ;—at last the day
Came round when he should send them both away,
And still it failed him—half unconscious then,
He made the Menelaus Adrien,

And something whispered him he knew not
  whence :
"Thou, if thou be an honest man get hence !"

XI.

Then winter vanished in a mist of rain,
And the world smiled to see the spring again :
Then first of all the flowers on the hill

The violet came, and soon the daffodil,
And in the valley by the torrent bed
One morning you might find the drooping head
Of a white narcissus-star above the grass,
Till in a little while you dared not pass
For fear of trampling them, and you would see
The crimson cup of that anemone,
The flower they say that sprang on Calvary,
And when long after Pisan galleys bore
The holy earth to this Italian shore
For all her dead to rest in, hither too
The seed came, and took heart in alien skies and grew.

And yet she went not as her wont had been
To find new flowers at morning, but between
Day-dawn and even bent above her books,
And went her way with over weary looks.
She needs a woman's sympathy, he thought,
Who waited on her least desire, and caught
Each rustling of her dress along the stone
Or faintest footfall far ; too much alone
We dwell here—seeing how she clung
To old Annita—for a child so young.

And in a little while it chanced there came
A letter from the North that told the fame
Of Anton's pictures; he had found at last,
They said, the note that failed him, and surpassed
Himself; his rumour was in every mouth—
"And yet," they said, "you linger in your South,
"But in the springtime you must make amends."

Then first of all since ever they were friends
One felt a touch of envy, no mere whim,
To watch her as she played at crowning him;
But a vague feeling he could not repress,
A fear he failed her somewhere, for success
Is ever sweet to woman; well he knew
The way to fame was easy for him too
Would he but choose it : but that might not be.
And what of Anton, could he choose but see
Why seemed her praises a reproach to hear ?
He dared not look into her eyes for fear
Of reading what he dreaded—and that day
He kept from sight of her, and turned away
When she came near to watch his work, and still
His mind was troubled with a boding ill.

He would have died sooner than not be true
To Adrien; and deep in his heart there grew
A shadow darkening, as he thought, a fear
For the undoing of two lives more dear
Than anything on earth; and it was so
His finer instinct could not choose but know
The meaning of her change.

    And it was this
His life had wanted, all he seemed to miss
That human touch, long out of reach, above
His art, was just this very need of Love.
Then all the best that was in him took fire,
Late learning Love, burned into one desire
To help her somehow, as Love longs to give
Its all on earth to one of all that live.
Only for him was nothing left to do
But leave her ere it be too late; he knew
There was no other way that he might choose,
And now seemed nothing left to win or lose
By all his triumphs, now men's praise or blame,
Success or failure were grown much the same.

She was so young, so innocently pure,
He dared persuade himself he was not sure
Of all he feared to picture ; but that dread
Mastered his self-control, therefore he said :
" My work is ended now, and I shall go
" North to our land this summer-time,—we grow
" Too straightened here."

                        He only heard her say :
" We shall be lonely when you go away."
But Adrien thought, so best, when Anton goes
She will be less constrained ; and when she rose
And came to ask him aught, and laid her hand
Upon his shoulder softly, and would stand
Waiting his answer, with love long deferred,
He pressed it softly, as a little bird
One must be gentle with, and drew her close,
And thought it will be well when Anton goes.

Ah ! what a world of things he recked not of
When he mistook her reverence for love.

XII.

Yet Anton lingered, and the weeks went by
Waiting to cast his Psyche. May drew nigh,
With still seas and returning nightingales,
Yet now they never set the painted sails
At moon-rise. Now she seldom cared to sing
As once she used, but it was grown to spring,
And still her cheek was paler. Yet he stayed
From day to day, and evermore delayed
The statue's casting; and now May was gone.

It was the day before the day whereon
He should go Northward; he was grown aware
Something had changed him, he could hardly bear
The look of Adrien's eyes, so trusting still,
So innocent of any boding ill,
Of any cloud between them, while he knew
His own heart's heart half loyal, half untrue.

And he could look into her soul and see;
For souls that love are quick to sympathy;

Her faith had all been centred on one truth
In fervent worship, all the dreams of youth,
All first ideals, all things holy and high
Seen with child-adoration, seemed to lie
With her as woman, dedicate above
To woman's self abandonment in Love.

The child of love, and nurtured on romance,
Rich with so fatal an inheritance,
Kept from the world's unfaith, a life apart,
Unwarped from trust and judging from the heart,
The one thing waited for was over-past,
And she had found out love too late at last.

Then he went forth and wondered all that day:
These many weeks he had known he must not stay,
But courage failed him, he had still deferred
The hour of parting, now he only heard
A little voice that cried—"too late, too late,"
"What hast thou done!"—And then in fierce self-
    hate
He cursed his weakness, he had meant to hide
His secret,—and, he thought—the world was wide,

Why were we thrown together—just we three
Of all that live and love? Why need it be
This one of all on earth, this only one?
Oh, fool! what hast thou done, what hast thou done!

We were so well together once, and fate
Has set between us—ah no, no, not hate!
Not hate, but needs division, oh, my friend,
My master, angel!—and is this the end
Of our ideals? Wherefore, oh, my God!
Was this the goal to which we slowly trod?
We—hand in hand—to where love cannot be
In the world evermore twixt me and thee!

He found a shepherd on the hills, and stayed
And talked with him a little while, and played
With the young kids; he could not be alone
With that intolerable monotone
Of Grilli in the ilex trees;—until
It grew near even, and across the hill
He watched them enter by the village gate—
And the far waves moaned to him, "Too late! too
    late!"

Alone still, hollow-hearted, seeing naught,
He wandered up and down, and thought, and thought
How should he live the morrow through and hide
This cursed thing from Adrien, and, blank-eyed,
Stared through the tree-trunks, where the setting sun
Burned red, and the waves wailed, "What hast thou
    done?"

And the sun stood one moment on the wave,
Then slowly sank, and day was in its grave;
And hope and faith and all things seemed to die.

But suddenly he came under the clear sky
Out of the gloom and mystery of the wood,
On the free hill-side; and awhile he stood
Just where he met them that first autumn eve;
Now he had done what tears could not retrieve
Or penitence atone, or years undo;
Had come between the trusting and the true,
And cursed the hand that blessed.
                Then faint and far
Beyond the rose-flush grew the evening star.

And the sky changed, the hills changed, and the sea,
Only that star beamed downward stedfastly,
Beamed through the twilight, till at last there stole
A white ray down that pierced into his soul,
Unbarred his heart, and made all wild thoughts cease
With sense of calm and permanence and peace,
And seemed to say, " one right, one light, one wrong,
" Too late is never though deferred too long,
" Do I not outshine many storms ! "

         And so
He changed his wavering purpose, he would go
To Adrien, speak out manfully and true,
And tell him all he dreaded, all he knew,
In expiation ;—and then go his way
For ever if need be, or till some day
They bade him come again—his mind was set,
And he was quite calm now—so they two met.

 And what he said !—only a long while they walked
The shore that evening, and talked on and talked
Gently and bravely, and so at the last

Took hands as men do who are moved, and passed
Together silent up into the tower.

And it was moonrise in a little hour.

Then Adrien; "Since to-morrow parts us two,
"Let us go out as we were used to do
"Once more across the sea, which has so long
"Cradled our dreams—let us sing one more song,
"We three together! Once more let us steer
"Along the moonpath as we did last year,
"Into the old dream-havens!"

                                  And so they
Went down the rock-path to the little bay,
And it was sultry under a clear sky—
Scirocco air, or thunder gathering nigh;
And the world seemed not sleeping, only still
And waiting; slowly through a rift of hill
Rose the wan moon beyond, and weirdly rang
The lute strings pausing to the song she sang :—

Sail and row! sail and row!
Where do the ships in the waters go?

Cloud or sun, cloud or sun,
All the ways of the ships are one.

Night and day, night and day,
Love's land looks over the waves alway.

Star and moon, star and moon,
Will guide us into the haven soon.

Moon and star! moon and star!
We have sailed and sailed, and it still is far.

Heart in heart, hand in hand,
But the bark was lost in sight of the land.

She knew not why she chose that song to sing,
Only upon the last line faltering
Laid the lute by, and would not sing again.
And Adrien watched her with a numbing pain,
Pale as the foam there in the pale moonlight.
And then she said, " Turn back now, for to-night
" I have a foolish dread ; it feels as though

" There lay a curse upon the world." And so
They turned and rowed in silence back to land.

And Anton said, " Good night." She felt his hand
Burn through her fingers, and she wondered why.
He said, " Good night ; it is not quite good-bye,
" For we have all to-morrow ere we part."

Then first she felt that something in her heart
Was severed—something gone for evermore ;
She could not see things clearly as before,
And the vague terror of some unknown sin
Changed all the stars, and darkened from within.
And scared as one that marches to his doom,
She went into her little raftered room
And stared across the silence. None to share
This wild foreboding that she could not bear
What might the morrow bring !

And then she dreamed
The room grew full of presences, it seemed
Those white-robed sisters drew to her bedside
And looked so loving, and so gentle-eyed,

Not one reproachful, as they would express
" From our safe haven are we come to bless ;
" You chose the world's way, sister, yet be brave
" For you chose well, and we are come to save
" Those wandering feet from falling," Then she
    knelt,
Reaching her arms towards them, and so felt
A hand upon her forehead, and heard one say,
" Child, when the heart is troubled, kneel and pray."
And one out in the shadow saw her rise,
With rain of tears in sorrow-wistful eyes,
And kneel on the cold marble, Adrien heard
Her prayer go skyward, weeping word by word :
For " Lord," she said, " the way is very steep
" And I have wandered far, thou, therefore, keep
" My feet from falling ; I am come between
" The noblest love of friendship ever seen,
" And I am bound to what I may not love,
" And what I love is out of reach above
" All earthly hope ; therefore, forgive my cry,
" It was so lonely that I longed to die.
" Now therefore, Lord, have pity on Thy child,
" Who seeks Thy mercy to be reconciled ;

"Therefore, forgive me if I dare to pray,
"Whose heart had wandered, Lord, so far away,
"For well I know it had I but loved Thee,
"Thy love would cast him out, and leave me free."
Then she lay down upon her little bed,
All her hair's gold entangled round her head;
And the young eyes were grown too tired to weep,
So gently closed, and then she fell on sleep,
And he still watched her in the shadow light.
Then he went out into the sultry night.
There was no stir of wind in any tree,
No faintest ripple on the glass-calm sea;
The very stars shone wanly overhead,
The worst was answered now, and all the world
    seemed dead.

XIII.

And Adrien wandered up and down the shore.

All ended now, and he might doubt no more;
The worst was answered; in his lonely breast
The last faint hope was dead with all the rest;—

That last faint hope we never dare let go,
When all the while we cannot choose but know
The golden thread is breaking, and cling fast,
To sink the deeper when it yields at last.

For now there was not any longer place
For hope, or chance of change; time might efface
Or kill, but could not alter; once, he knew,
Love dawns, once only to be pure and true;
And he had girt this young life round with dreams,
And she had grown to him as one who seems
Out of earth's reach to tarnish, shrined above
With the high things he had held worthy love
To live and die for; he had set her there
In his heart's heart, and kept that image fair
From chance and changing things, like some white star,
Serene, far over where the storm-clouds are,
To consecrate all labours, and to make
His every effort holier for her sake;
And he had seemed so near to winning this,
This too great gladness, that such love was his
To be a glory on the path he trod,
To rest about him as the breath of God.

They might outlive this,—might, long years away,
Grow somewhat nearer in an after day;
But that young life, with all its noon unspent,
To droop at morning! He had been content
To bear his lot in silence, for man's best
In pain is perfected, and little rest
From the long struggle comes to any man
The way he journeys since his years began.
But this young life,—he could not set it free;
Man binds and love rebels, and he must see,
Day after day, the love she could not hide,
Not his, another's, fettered to his side.
There is some sorrow that defies control,
The bitterness of death was on his soul,—
And a long while he stared across the sea,
And thought, and thought, If I could set her free!

He had not marked a small dark cloud that rose
Over the sea-line eastward, how it grows,
And veils the stars, and overshades the light
Of that round moon, how sultry lies the night
On the unrippled waters—heavily,
Great drops fall plashing on the darkened sea.

He stole into the chamber where she slept,
And sorrow overflowed, quite close he crept
And watched her sleep; she dreamed and never knew
How wild without the storm of summer grew.
He closed the casement, for the rain fell cold,
And ever and again the thunder rolled,
From crag to answering echo, long and loud—
Flashed down the sky from jaggèd cloud to cloud
God's anger written in the writhing flame!
And yet she wakened not, he breathed her name,
But she was dreaming, and no answer came.

So a long hour he lingered at her side
Lest she should waken, till the echoes died
Beyond the hills, and through the window bars
Shone out once more the cloudless maze of stars;
And all the memories of days gone by
Came one by one, old hopes that once were high,
And the glad days that they had spent together
When first he found love in the summer weather,
And love had brought him hither to this last.

Slowly and silently the hours passed;
And ever and again this thought would grow—

"But now, if I should chance upon them so,
"That hand of his that once I trusted there
"Upon my golden, my own golden hair,
"And all her spirit laughing up to his
"Through those great eyes of her, ah, God! and this
"My friend, my more than brother, and this—but no,
"The very thought were treason—sweet, not so,
"For very loyal are they both to me,
"God knows and love knows that could never be!
"Oh little lonely life I tried to fold
"Into my arms to keep, you only told
"Your love to God, in that white prayer you prayed."
No taint of self was in his thoughts, no shade
Of least reproach, once more he learned, the price
Of Love on earth is weighed in sacrifice.

And slowly, silently the night went by,
His heart was breaking, and he could not die.
Then he knelt down, and prayed, as one, indeed,
Scarce knowing what he prayed for, only the need
And craving of spirit to communicate
With strength, and light, and what is more than fate,
To ease this deadly chillness of despair,

And as he looked out on the twilight air
The slow dawn grew in answer to his prayer.
  And then he turned and looked on her again,
So calm in sleep, so guiltless of his pain,
Sleep lay so sweetly on her, as a child
That dreaming smiles, so in her dream she smiled.
The fair young neck lay bare, all round her head
The golden ripple of her hair was shed,
And one white hand was on her heart at rest,
And rose with every beating of her breast.
The finger was unclasped whereon was set
His opal ring he gave when first they met;
Only he thought the stone had lost its hue,
And gently kneeling at her side he drew
The golden circle from her hand, and yet
She did not wake,
                The stars were well-nigh set,
And the still dawn grew paler; then he rose
And went and dressed in the rough seaman's clothes.
The fisher's sash that he had worn that day
When first he anchored in the lonely bay
And found her singing in the olive wood.
Once more he came, and at her side he stood.

And gazed and gazed, as though he strove to trace
In his heart's heart the image of that face
For ever and for ever,—then bent low,
And yet a moment watching, lingered so;
In maiden sleep so very pure and fair,
He pressed one kiss upon her tangled hair,
And turned and went, and never looked behind.

If one had seen him then unmoved, resigned;
He seemed as they whose peace is made
With days and years, who wait till the last shade
Clouds o'er the eyes.—Death in the heart may be,
But love had found its own eternity.

Then he went down into the little bay,
By the old path, and it was early day,
And the long grass was silvered with the dew,
And the birds sang as ever. But he drew
The old boat shorewards—wind enough to fill
The painted sail—and, from the shadowy hill,
He passed beyond into the gold sun's track,
Southward and Southward, and not once looked back.

And when the sun was well above the tower
Féda awoke; the passing thunder shower

Had cleared the heavy air, and the new day
Breathed sweet and fresh about her as she lay.
The song of birds made gladness in the air,
And God, she thought, has surely heard my prayer.
For youth's deep sleep had eased her weariness.

Lighter of heart she rose, and chose the dress
He praised her in, and braided up her hair
For his sake, and was glad that she was fair.
Now she had conquered—he should never know.

But by the window in the hall below,
Alone stood Anton, waiting ; and his head
Was bent above a written page he read ;
And she looked up in that pale face of his
For greeting ;
        Then she saw the lines he read
Were Adrien's writing, and no word was said.

" To Anton and to Féda one short word,
" And then let me keep silence ! God has heard
" One prayer of yesternight. To you, old friend,
" She comes, a child yet, yours till these days end,
" Else had not this been possible. Your tears

" Will keep my memory green a few short years,
" The rest have long forgotten ;—all is said,
" You had one friend once, Anton : he is dead.
" And you, my love, and, ever my love, although
" Our ways in life divide hence, and I go.
" Love him for ever, only ; and be ye
" Too rich in joy to waste one thought on me !
" For now, because when the old hope was sweet,
" The waters used to bear me to your feet.
" I turn again to the old kindly sea,
" And my own love will be enough for me.
" The time is very short to death from birth,
" And I have much to do in the wide earth,
" Whom now the silence covers.   Let the dead
" Sleep on !   Love well !   Be happy !   All is said
" In this, that you will see my face no more
" In any way of any sea or shore."

    Three times she read it wholly through and through
And could not speak to question, and she knew
The eyes that watched were brimming with hot tears,
And tremblingly she stood, as one who hears
His doom of death, and is half glad to die.

By this the sun was high in the pale sky,
And from its place in the dark bay below
The boat was gone, and ah, how long ago!
But the birds sang as alway, and the foam
Splashed up against the red rocks of their home,
And the sunflowers waved in the light breeze.

Then suddenly as one who watching sees
The last faint smile upon a dying face
Before death closes o'er, a moment's space
They saw through tear-dimmed eyes that strained away,
How, in the golden promise of the day,
A small white sail was fading in the South.

Then Anton stooped and kissed her on the mouth.

XIV.

And neither spoke.
   All that long morning through,
He sat there by the window, hardly knew
The passing hours, self-tortured, till she came
To his side softly and so breathed his name.

Then he looked up and saw her, scarcely known,
So changed since yester even, only grown
Spiritually beautiful; the grace
Of inspiration on an angel-face
Seemed lightening in her eyes, as one awoke
From childhood into life or death.   She spoke.

" This hour must part us two for ever; nay,
" No word!   This is no easy thing to say.
" Someday, with calmer insight, you will know
" I loved you well enough to dare to go,
" And save your soul and mine.   Dear, we must keep
" To the old holdfasts knowing not how deep
" The thornless way might lead us.   Hear me yet!
" The past is past and gone beyond regret;
" I have undone the very noblest life
" Now living.—Yet no less am I his wife
" Here in the world for evermore.   Nay, dear,
" We cannot alter this.   I see more clear,
" Because I love you better than my peace,
" The bond is bound, and there is no release.
" Better to suffer silent all life through,
" Than do a deed to hunger to undo

" For ever and ever ! Shall not death atone
" Life's failure ? Now will I go back alone
" To the good sisters, they will take me in,
" And I will live remission of my sin.

" And you, for this last charge of love I lay
" Upon you, for my sake, by night by day,
" Rest not for ever till sometime, somewhere
" You find him living, and I have no fear
" But you will find him, if you seek where'er
" Some human wrong is crying for redress,
" Some human need for love ; and you will bless
" The very pain that puts our souls apart,
" And be as once you were. And now, dear heart,
" This one thing yet I pray you, stir not hence
" Until to-morrow, I shall send you thence
" A certain message ; so shall you be freed
" To start upon my quest. Farewell, God speed !
" For I shall never look you in the face
" Till I can meet you in the spiritual place,
" With no least cloud between us.—We shall tell
" The rest hereafter,—only now, farewell ! "

But he bent low in self-abasement, heard,
And touched her hand, and answered not a word.
He had no will but hers, and he would do
Her bidding now and ever; for he knew
There was no other way; but he would make
His life's atonement living for her sake.
And when he looked to bless her she was gone,
And he was left in the wide world alone,
Till love in life imprisoned find release.

Only the Psyche lives—a masterpiece
Of sculpture, so men say;—the type of love
Unmarred by passion, winged to pass above
Into those highest havens dimly dreamed,
Where hope and faith that trusted are redeemed,
Whence sometimes, as from lost skies overcast,
And clearer, surer as we hold it fast,
This best is whispered to sad souls that pray,
"Somewhere, an' thou be true, somewhere, some day."

LYRICS.

*I heard a bird sing in a leafless tree
In bleak midwinter—and it gladdened me;*

*Sing out for joy that noon forbore to freeze,
Or one stray sunbeam struck adown the trees,*

*Some wintry greenness,—such a little thing
Had touched its heart to gratitude to sing:*

*The world was grey, the woods were bare and sad,
But I was better that the bird was glad:*

*And then I thought ways are that ever lie
Far off from summer in a clouded sky,*

*To seek the gladness, to accept the sign,
Might strike a light to darker lives than mine,*

*So seeking sing I in the wintry way,
So singing seek to gladden whom I may.*

THE JOURNEY HOME.

Deep into the night we flew, through the great plains broadening far
To the South of hills and the North of seas, low under the moon and star.

And we scared with a midnight shriek the slumbering haunts of men,
Dived into the gloom of forests, whirled out by river and fen.

On and away, and ever away, through the night like a moving flame,
Till the folk have a different speech, and the lands have another name!

We had left the cloud in our wake, the sky had been overcast,
But here was the moon stood still, and the world went wildering past:

And there grew such a sense of space, like a prisoner's
    suddenly freed,
In that slumberous rest of motion, safe borne on the
    wings of speed;

And the silvery greys of midnight, the shadowy land
    the stream,
Grew part with the phantom pictures twixt sleep and
    a waking dream.

So the night went by and a wave of light gained over
    us while we sped,
The stars went down in the rosy wave and the wester-
    ing shadows fled:

A wide opalescent water lay blanched in the dawn
    mists dim,
And the blaze of the advent day grew flame on the
    eastward rim:

The work of the world began for team and harrow
    and hind,
The smoke curled up from the farm-house roof and
    mixed with the morning wind.

Then we came to a world of meadows, a pastoral land of kine,
The meads were greyed with the early dew, the poplars waved in a line;

The grazing cattle looked up to stare as over their plains we flew,
Their bells rang crisp in the morning chill, you could see their tracks in the dew.

Then the hills began, and the covert side, and the pear and the apple tree,
And here and there was a village spire, with a life we shall never see.

We stayed by a town stream-girded with gardens green to the marge,
And labouring men unloading red tiles from a resting barge,

With bleaching linen, the white and brown that flapped on a line in the breeze,
And carts laid up in the central street, and avenue rows of trees;

It was easy to see it was market-day, the folk were in
    market blouse,
There were booths and stalls and clatter of life, and
    chatter of homely news;

Then on by the factory piles that loom on the further
    side,—
A passing look at their little world, a moment's glance
    from the wide;

So into a wild waste land all fen and willow and reed,
With sickly shallows and aspens fret, and wilderness
    isles of weed,

And I think there are clouds that ever shut out that
    waste from the sky,
That the bats wheel there in the nightly mists, and
    the owl has a haunt hard by,

And the wraiths of some doom forgotten must wail on
    the midnight air,
For the curse on yon tower of ruin half hid in the
    aspens bare.

So on and away, and ever away, and noon by now in
    the sky,
On and away, and ever away, till the end of the land
    draws nigh.

Oh, surely those are the sand-hills where the river
    broadens away
To masts of ships in the distance, white sails in the
    light mid-day;

And these blown trees are the hardy sign of a land
    where the winds are free,
And surely this is the dear salt breath that only
    breathes from the sea!

Lo, one great sheen to the east and west the luminous
    waters roll,
With a light of joy and a breeze of strength to the
    long land-prisoned soul!

O beautiful ship with the dipping prow bound over
    the space between,
There are fairer hills on the further side and meads of
    a deeper green!

We are close to the old cliff walls washed white of
    the ocean foam ;
The masts of the ships have an English flag, and this
    is the island home !

And here are the friends who wait me, the ready to
    take my part,
The quick to help me and understand, the loyal and
    true of heart.

Oh, when and where shall I ever go out to you all as
    I would,
And receive you into myself and be and become your
    good !

Now God speed all that are far from home, and bring
    them again at last
To the fair green isle in the ocean's arms when
    wandering days are past,

For though I have given all lands my love and all folk
    under the sky,
There was never a man that loved her yet with a
    greater love than I.

ALBANO.

The lake lies calm with its mountain crown,
    And the twilight star shows clear,
And large and solemn it gazes down
    In the mirror of the mere.
Was it here they rowed in their crazy craft,
    Where only the ripples are,—
The strange lake-folk of the floating raft?
    Was it yesterday? said the star.

And the mountains slept, and the nights fell still,
    And the thousand years rolled by.
Was there once a city on yon low hill,
    With its towers along the sky,
And the cries of the war-din of long ago
    Wailed over the waters far?
There is no stone left for a man to know
    Since yesterday, said the star.

And the mountains sleep and the ripples wake,
　　And again a thousand years,
And the tents of battle are by the lake,
　　And the gleam of the Norsemen's spears;
They bend their brows with a fierce surmise
　　On the lights in the plain afar,
And the battle-hunger is in their eyes.
　　Was it yesterday? said the star.

And a thousand years,—and the lake is still,
　　And the star beams large and white,
The burial chant rolls down the hill,
　　Where they bury the monk at night;
The mountains sleep and the ripples lave
　　The shore where the pine-woods are,
And there's little change but another grave
　　Since yesterday, said the star.

REVERIE.

AN ITALIAN NIGHT.

LONELY here by starry midnight, with the springtide's mellow moon
Waning to the birth of summer's, and the May nights into June;
Chime of convent bells dies faintly down the moon-enchanted air,
Leaves to nightingales the silence, waking music everywhere;
Through the dark of ilex shadows, where the fire-flies pause and pass,
Steal along with noiseless footfall on the violets in the grass!
Listen, listen, what mad rapture! and the song seems very near,
Moonbeams striking through the shadow light the woodland hollow clear
Where the antique marble Ceres stands serenely calm and cold,
Watching moon by moon for ever how her ilex trees grow old.

Sharp against the sky's blue twilight, heaving throat and drooping wings,
Little head uplifted starward, how it sings, and sings, and sings !
Thrice the deep-repeated sole-note, and a breathing space, and then
That wild ecstasy of answer, and the whole song through again.
And you did not fear the statue ; have you watched it there so long
Night by night its still unheeding of the transport of your song?
Cold is she, of stone and heartless, underneath her ilex tree,
I am true, and warm, and loving, but you would not come to me ;
We must stand far from you alway, wonder alway spring by spring,
What it is in starry midnight moves your little hearts to sing ;
Stand apart for all our longing from these lonely lives of birds,

Never wholly know the secret of the song that has no words.
One there was in old Assisi, in the world they call him Saint,
Last of men who knew your language and made answer to your plaint;
Gentle spirits since have loved you, but the world's mistrust is more,
And we know not as they knew you in the golden time before.
Yet sing on, so I may hearken,—growing part with the still scene,
With the darkly waving branches and the stars that look between.

For thou makest all times equal singing that same antique tune,
Thou, and these old trees and Ceres, and the star-orbs and the moon.
Who are these in long procession winding down the wooded hill,
Thronging noiseless on the twilight—and the bird is singing still?

Phantoms of the airy fancy, yet I see them near and near,
Ghosts that glide along the shadows—canst thou conjure spirits here?
Unfamiliar forms and faces—hast thou stolen these from time?
Re-arisen strange and lovely, dwellers of the world's young prime!
Garb and mien of pastoral people of the old Etruscan line,
Fathers of the grim-walled city on yon spur of Apennine!
They are gathering round the goddess, and thou singest undeterred.
Seest thou not the long procession—art thou too a phantom bird?
Wreathing ghostly garlands round her, and across thy song I hear
Clashing of the sacred cymbals and deep lowing of the steer;
And the maids unbind the fillets and their hair floats down the breeze,

Softly traced like summer moon-clouds on the darkness of the trees,
And the youths take up the reed-pipes, I can hear them shrill and strong
Blown across dim wastes of silence in the changes of thy song.
All the arms are straining upwards in the old sweet use of prayer,
Swells the spirit chorus loud and louder on the startled air!
Glides a shadow o'er the moonlight—where are all those spirits flown?
Waken, dreamer, from thy dreaming! for that voice was but thine own!
Waken, dreamer, from thy dreaming! thou hast scared the nightingale
Into deeper, leafier coverts far away along the vale!
Over yon mist-halo'd mountains grows a light that dims the star,
Havened in the topmost rock-crests, where the winter snows yet are;

Pales the blue to green and golden, hues that herald
    home the sun
Lingering yet on Asian waters—but his sister's reign
    is done;
I will mount up from the valley, through the olives
    and the vines,
Meet the sunrise on the mountains in the sweet scent
    of the pines,
Watch the morning mists roll upward from the silver-
    winding streams,
Summer grows and day dawns early, and the night is
    short for dreams.

NIGHT VOICES.

Row no more now, stay thy hand,
    Only drift along and dream ;
What voices of the stranger land
    Float singing o'er the stream !
Under yon low-shadowed shore
Mingles song with plash of oar,
    Stay a moment, row no more !

Ruddy lights gleam here and there
    Where the quiet hamlets are,—
Folk whose songs are sweet to hear
    Under summer night and star,—
Row no more, the stream is strong
Swift, too swift we drift along,
    Let us linger with the song !

Freshens breeze and on the prow
    Beat the ripples rushing by,
Faint the voices echo now ;—
    Glides a glimmer up the sky,

Then a cloud grows silver-lined,
Mountain edges more defined,
    Somewhere lurks the moon behind :

Dies the last shrill note away,—
    Row once more now, row once more :
We must pass, and these must stay
    On their own low-shadowed shore ;
Rovers of the world are we,
Murmur not that thou art free
    Till the river finds the sea.

PRAGUE.

Moldau bends, and ripples broader
    Underneath the citied ridge,
Sculptured saint and hero-warder
    Guard the many-statued bridge.

Yonder rise the domes and gables,
    Halls of half-forgotten kings,—
Sounds of names that move like fables
    O'er a tide of human things.

Here were banquetings assembled,
    Haughty speech and flow of wine,
When the Northern princes trembled
    At the name of Wallenstein.

Friedland's palace! That world's wonder,
    Can it be this sombre pile,
Where the stucco cracks asunder
    And the frescoes make you smile?

This the tower where your hero
    Gauged the boding star's intent,
Cabalistic plus and zero
    Mark the nothing that it meant.

Princes feared and armies praised him,
    Bigots blessed and mothers cursed,
Till the ruin sank that raised him,
    And his creatures struck him first.

Meteor of a tumult season
    Flashed across the troubled skies,
Giant gifts and human treason—
    Not a hero in my eyes.

I will seek a corner rather
    Which I came to Prague to find,
Holds a thought which pierces farther
    Through a less romantic mind.

Deep in narrow streets and crowded,
    Where it reeks of slums and stews,
Cells and garrets darkness-shrouded,
    Is the Quarter of the Jews;

In the heart of the old city
    Walled away from living tread,
Out of date of human pity,
    Lies the rest-close of their dead.

Alders never a bird would nest in
    Shake a few leaves blown and sere;
Only grass will grow protesting
    Something left of nature here!

Ah! the grim tombs closely serried,
    Weirdly leaning moss-o'ergrown!
Here five deep the dead are buried
    Underneath the weight of stone:

Each of these a life recorded,
    Human soul that agonized,
Outcasts all and over-lorded,
    And forsaken and despised!

Bound in narrow bonds enclosing,
    Here they lived and toiled and died,
Here at last were laid reposing,—
    In the wall the suicide.

Stedfast stood they man by brother,
    Asked no mercy, fought their fight,
Drawing closer each to other
    In the dark and angry night.

Lightly olden sorrows move us,
    Needs the near to seem the true,
Howsoe'er these stones reprove us,
    We shall fail of pity's due.

We should plant you round with flowers,
    You grim army of grey stones,
Feed your want of love with ours,
    And revere the ancient bones.

Exiles in the stormy haven,
    Sleepless in the wakeless bed,
Could I read the story graven
    On these annals of your dead,

Would it speak out stern and scorning
    Of the burden long endured,
Left behind to meet the morning,
    And the triumphing assured?

Let me deem the graven stone meant
    Surely triumph more than pain,
And that need of our atonement
    May be less by this your gain!

Rugged types of lives heroic,
    'Tis enough, the wild grass waves,
And a glory mute and stoic
    Crowns your unforgotten graves.

THE SKYLARKS.

OH the sky, the sky, the open sky
   For the home of a song-bird's heart!
And why, why, and forever why,
   Do they stifle here in the mart:
Cages of agony, rows on rows,
Torture that only a wild thing knows:
   Is it nothing to you to see
That head thrust out through the hopeless wire,
And the tiny life, and the mad desire
   To be free, to be free, to be free?
Oh the sky, the sky, the blue wide sky
   For the beat of a song-bird's wings!
And why, why and forever why,
   Is the only song it sings.

Great sad eyes with a frightened stare,
Look through the 'wildering darkness there,
   The surge, the crowd, and the cry;
Fluttering wild wings beat and bleed,

And it will not peck at the golden seed,
    And the water is almost dry:
Straight and close are the cramping bars
From the dawn of mist to the chill of stars,
    And yet it must sing or die!
Will its marred harsh voice in the city street
    Make any heart of you glad?
It will only beat with its wings and beat,
    It will only sing you mad.

Better to lie like this one dead,
Ruffled plumage of breast and head,
Poor little feathers for ever furled,
Only a song gone out of the world!

Where the grasses wave like an emerald sea,
    And the poppies nod in the corn,
Where the fields are wide and the wind blows free,
    This joy of the spring was born,
Whose passionate music loud and loud
    In the hush of the rose of morn,
Was a voice that fell from the sailing cloud
    Midway to the blue above,—

A thing whose meaning was joy and love,
Whose life was one exquisite outpouring
   Of a sweet surpassing note,
And all you have done is to break its wing,
   And to blast God's breath in its throat!

   If it does not go to your heart to see
The helpless pity of those bruised wings,
The tireless effort with which it clings
   To the strain and the will to be free,
I know not how I shall set in words
   The meaning of God in this,
For the loveliest thing in this world of His
   Are the ways and the songs of birds.
But the sky, the sky, the wide free sky
   For the home of the song-bird's heart!
And why, why and forever why,
   Do they stifle here in the mart?

RICHARD WAGNER.

In sea-born Venice, while the shadows crept
   Across the ripples of the still Lagoon,
   And even gathered on the waning noon,
Death kissed his forehead, and the master slept.

His hand had never faltered from its best,
   Nor his strength wearied, nor his eye grown dim;
   But in the quiet noon death came to him,
And now—we must not envy him his rest.

His path was like the mountain torrent's, hurled
   Through crags and gullies, bursting to be free—
   To calm and broaden as it neared the sea
And rest upon the bosom of the world.

He felt the storm break round him—let them rave!
   This is the burthen of the sons of song;
   He cast on time the verdict—not for long
The shafts of envy beat upon the grave.

He gave youth, life, to labour stern and true,
   Knowing the night is longer than the day:
   Short rest they take upon their onward way,
Those fiery spirits that achieve the new.

But restful now and very calm he lies,
   Who woke strange chords to passion, strong to reach
   The sense of things which lie too deep for speech—
That music only may eternalise.

Death and decay are not for him, nor tears,
   But strength and beauty, and eternal prime:
   A giant soul that lies abroad on time,
A voice for ever in the march of years.

The master is not, but the spirit breathes;
   He heeds not now what flowers we may shed;
   Yet on that grave, in homage to the dead,
Let mine be cast among the laurel wreaths!

VICTOR HUGO.

How shall we reverence the great soul dead?
Oh, not with tears, for he was old and tired,
And mutely welcome as a friend desired
Death laid the laurel on that ancient head;
And rightly well Death kissed those brows
   In the fair year-time between
The moon of flowering lilac boughs
   And the full summer green.
So unwithstood, so painlessly
   The mystic summons stole
And stayed the royal heart, set free
   That elemental soul.

How shall we yield him homage in his death!
This was a man eyed with a starry faith
That sees beyond the temporal dream, and knows
The Possible of God,—therefore, he chose
The upward, onward;—Prophet, with song's voice
Crying, the world is glorious, rejoice!
Crying, the pain is finite here, retrieve!
Crying, the soul is infinite, believe!

This man made Truth his altar, by man's birth
Proclaimed man's right to joy; ceased not cry
The reign of falsehood has an end on earth,
Upward and on!—And therefore, when the lie
Gauded itself in purple, and when men fell down
To worship, this man's voice rose fearless high
And smote in lightning-flashes on the crown,
Accepting exile rather than renown;
Therefore, among the crownless kings
    Write him the unsubdued,
The lyrist of all human strings,
    The voice of herohood.

This man was stern and tender, strong and mild:
The hero heart is nearest to the child;
He had the tears for human things, the touch
On mortal sorrow that availeth much:
For him was no man unredeemed or lost,
But love was lavished where the need was most:
This man took up the very outcast's shame
With such an echo that its note struck deep
Into the soul of Pity, and became
The poet pleader of all those that weep.

This man loved all things gentle, children's eyes
And maiden whiteness and young motherhood;
Call him the tolerant and the wise!
Call him the human and the good!
He did not use his gift of song
To lie adrowze in meadows green,
And wail about what might have been,
His note was this,—redeem the wrong,
The fairest crowns were ever given
   Are innocence and mirth,
Leave God to work in heaven,
   Work thou with love on earth!

He knew the mother nature, sang aloud
Light of the sun and shadow of the cloud;
He used the eagle's wing for his song's flight,
He took the thunder in his lips to smite,
He had the rock's resistance and the sea's
Glory of change, and the wind's melodies.
He waited till the days grew long,
Till May brought back the morning song;
And now his spirit's wings that seemed
   To beat against the bars,

May wander where his daring dreamed
　　From world to world of stars.

How shall we honour the great soul that's dead?
Oh, not this strife and clamour,—" Peace," he said!
Join heart and hand, forbear to rave
Your petty strife at such a grave;
What matter where the mourners lay
The mask from which he fled away?
Take up his word and echo strong
His triumph-note for burial song,
Where human hearts are, there world-wide
His grave is with the glorified.

THE NATURE-CHILD.

Too soon, too soon the others
    Were startled out of rest,
This child was Nature-mother's,
    And long lay in her breast.

Men shall not bind his going,
    And he shall dwell alone,
And yet not lonely, knowing
    The whole world for his own.

He shall be at peace with flowers,
    And know the songs of birds,
And Nature's secret powers,
    And tell it all in words.

He shall be warmed with summers,
    And fed on gentle rains,
And know for after-comers
    Such amplitude remains;

He shall be in the windless trances
    That hold the summer noons,
And range with the star dances,
    And wander with the moons;

And he shall walk at even
    With the wind along the sea,
And draw the clouds from heaven,
    And darken shudderingly,

And lash the dim waves under
    To threatening monster forms,
And roar out with the thunder,
    And be the soul of storms.

His shall be wandering places
    Unwalked of earthly feet,
In the sky's dreamy spaces,
    Where light and twilight meet,

And there the shadowy meaning
    Of things not clear to sight,
Through twilight intervening
    Shall pass up into light.

And all dumb things shall love him,
    And cast aside their fears;
And children's ways shall move him
    To laughter and to tears;

And he will hold them dearest
    Who best can understand,
Because their lives are nearest
    The Nature mother-land.

He shall feel the heart of nations,
    And see far things to be,
And pass through revelations
    To deeper mystery.

He shall absorb all changes,
    Perceiving naught is new,
And these the wider ranges
    Of old truths ever true.

He shall know all songs were fashioned
    Before the dawn of time,
Which poets, keenly passioned,
    Interpret into rhyme.

He shall learn his lofty duty
  To mediate with earth,
And in the womb of beauty
  Beget the second birth.

And none shall be too lowly,
  Too loveless to recall,
But love make all things holy,
  And love be unto all;

And souls that crave for pardon
  Shall come to him and find
A heart no sin can harden,
  A gentle voice and kind,

A gentle voice of reason
  That falls like April rain,
And thaws the winter's treason
  For hope to grow again.

He shall not seek for guerdon,
  Nor murmur at his years,
Content to bear life's burden,
  And reconciled with tears:

He shall know the highest gladness
   Is very near to pain,
That never human sadness
   Was wasted or in vain;

He shall learn the mystic union
   That is twixt souls and things,
And dwell in that communion,
   And fashion words to wings—

To wings that men may borrow,
   And follow where he trod,
To the sympathy with sorrow
   That is the joy of God.

And Time shall not estrange him
   To trustfulness and truth;
The years shall hardly change him,
   Nor bear away his youth;

But at the last awaking,
   His upward-straining eyes
Shall know the morning breaking
   Across familiar skies:

And he shall wake from sleeping
   As gently as at birth,
To fields of fairer reaping
   Than any fields of earth.

"I KNEW A POET."

I KNEW a poet,—one with eyes of laughter,
    A face like a sun-smile, eager as a boy,
Singing as the birds sing, trusting the hereafter—
    I knew a poet, and his name was Joy!

I knew a poet, who had eyes for beauty
    Piercing the cloud-mists, reaching over death,
Sounding the world's song like a hymn of duty,—
    I knew a poet, and his name was Faith!

One there was also gentle as a woman,
    Walking the sunless alleys of the city,
One all-compassionate, eloquently human,—
    I knew a poet, and his name was Pity!

But these with their loveless tissue of fair weaving,
    These with the joyless musical refrain,
These letting life go blind, and unbelieving,
    These looking earthward only and in vain;

These that have lain in the poppy-flowers waving,
    Grown where the fields turn wilderness and bare,
These with the look-back and the lotus craving,
    These with the thin self-echo of despair;

These ever straining after days that were not,
    These with their reckless abandonment of youth,
These that restrain not, wonder not, revere not,—
    These are no poets, or I know no Truth.

LYRICS.

I.

The form in which her spirit moved
    Was like her spirit fair,
The dwelling of a soul that loved,
    As innocent as prayer:

And but to know her was to pray
    Those young unclouded eyes
Might never see the world's highway,
    And only watch the skies.

II.

Though I be half of common clay,
    And half of light sea foam,
Though you are near the sun-ray,
    And the azure is your home,

The changing cloud renews its birth,
    And when the tear-drops rain,
You cannot choose but come to earth
    To get to heaven again.

III.

Two flowers in a world's garden,
   In the dark shadow one,
And one through noons of springtide
   Drawn up to see the sun.

Young flower of life, blow sun-ward
   To skies of summer blue!
But I that dwell in the shadow,
   What have I to do with you!

IN WINTER.

Heavy clouds in the waning light,
Flakes are falling feather-white,
Dreary gusts of winter blow,—
   Close your window to the snow!

Bright and light looks all within
Now the stormy days begin,
Shadows there flit to and fro,—
   Close your window to the snow!

Moans the night-wind o'er the wide,
Love will hold you safe inside,
Through the falling flakes I go,—
   Close your window to the snow!

SPRING'S PARDON.

Out of the sun came a spirit forth
    And whispered a word in my ear,
The winds went home to the frozen North,
    And the green broke over the sere:
The great clouds dreamed in the April blue,
And the spirit of love made all things new;
The whole world shook with a smile of glee,
For the songs you hear from the hawthorn tree,
    The scents that the branches wave you,
And my heart sang out as a bird set free,
For the spirit of spring took hold on me,
    And surely, I forgave you!

"THE PITY OF IT."

A TINY mound of grassy earth,
    And whose no word to tell,—
The little life was hardly worth
    Recording when it fell.
The birthright Joy it never found,—
    A cold and hungry hearth,
The city street for playing ground,
    And not the flower-path.
An autumn wind that blew too soon
    Unheeded bore away
The butterfly whose life's one noon
    Fell on a cloudy day.

TO ———

Tears to weep! and a world so green,
    And summer in all the air,—
A world God made to be joyful in,
    And a heart so near despair;
What can I do for thee, breaking heart?
Sorrow and thou must sit apart!

Heart, there is this that I can see,
    Only this to assign to gain,
That we do but learn what our joy might be
    Through the consciousness of pain:
Now it may be pain is the price we pay
For the glimpse of a joy we shall have some day.

SONG.

A THOUGHT that fell in the year's young prime,
    But I know not whence or where,—
A dream of a world in the blossom time
    With the bird's joy in the air :
When we were alone, we two, and young,
And the life to be was a song unsung;
Where the flower fields and the orchard trees
    Made a paradise of the down,
And away beyond were the purple seas
    And the tiny red-roofed town ;
The blossom shone and the birds were gay,
It was early noon of a month of May.

There was milk-white blossom and pale red pink,
    And dark red roofs by the shore ;—
And it seemed no dream, but as when we think
    Of a child-joy gone before,—
And you were dressed in the bridal white
With the years rolled back and the heart grown light.

Oh, world of blossom and purple sea,
    And green earth under the sun!
Oh, sweet little feet that walked with me,
    And true hands linked in one!
Ah, once in a life if a dream came true,
If a broken blossom could bloom anew!

GOOD-BYE.

TO A CHILD.

Good night, and wings of angels
    Beat round your little bed,
And all white hopes and holy
    Be on your golden head!

You know not why I love you,
    You little lips that kiss;
But if you should remember,
    Remember me with this;

He said that the longest journey
    Was all on the road to rest;
He said the children's wisdom
    Was the wisest and the best;

He said there was joy in sorrow
    Far more than the tears in mirth,
And he knew there was God in heaven,
    Because there was Love on earth.

A MEMORY.

I wish I could hear you laugh again, just one
Clear ring, your finger pointed in fun
In the unconstrained sweet way that took
The room with a ripple of life, and shook
The mind's cobwebs, in the merry play
That suffered no word of mine gainsay
Its shrill resistance;—then, I would wait
Till the storm was over, and grave as fate
Ignore the imperious child-behest,
Point out the flaw in your reason's best,
Reprove till the beautiful eyes grew sad,
As it needed penance to have been glad,
And the vehement mouth lost all its mirth
In the loveliest smile I have seen on earth,
Till you came to accord with your warm word,
      "friend,"
And took my word on your lips to blend
With a touch of yourself that made it new,
And felt more keenly, and twice as true,
And the way for the world was the way we knew.

Now I wonder, child, as the days grow old,
Is the laugh as loud, are the lips as bold,
Is the heart as warm and the life as glad,
The pity as quick and the smile as sad?
And if ever you think of the graver eyes
That stayed your riot of swift replies,
And calmed the torrent, the while they blest
The keen life-throbbing of your unrest!
And what you do as the days go by,
And think, and whether you learn as I
That the new dreams pass and the old remain!
And I wish I could hear you laugh again!

A NOCTURNE OF CHOPIN.

Gusts of the night-wind, loud and loud,
    Flickering lights on a friendless plain,
    Dimmed and lost in the driving rain,
Starless revel of storm and cloud,
Dark tree-lines on the ridge before,
    Steeps to climb with a weary will,
And ridges beyond and o'er and o'er—
        Peace, be still!
Stedfast yet through the rack o'erhead
Gleams the moon in her ring of red,
    Far away where the earth-storms cease;
    Far in the quiet, calmly there,
    Gleams the moon like a dream of peace,
        Someday, somewhere!

Faces, faces, wandering past,
    Never the face that by sea or shore
    Sought for ever I see no more,—
Loveless faces, leaves in the blast!
Night is dark and it's long till day—
These are the lips that kiss to kill,

And they whisper low and they smile alway—
    Peace, be still!
Clear and true in my heart I know
Smiles the face that I long for so,
    Whispers low, till the exile cease,—
        Surely I wait thee, surely there,
Where the wandering feet shall rest in peace,
    Someday, somewhere!

What is it, ever I hear you say,
    Mocking echo that would seem true?
    Hope, is there any for me and you?
How should I see you hidden away
Dead and buried and long ago?
    Only night-mists grey and chill,
Only the drowning storm-winds blow,—
    Peace, be still!
Over the world's voice clear and true
Wins the soul of a voice I knew;
    Wins and wins till the storm-throes cease;
        Surely I wait thee, surely there,
Where the night of doubt has a dawn of peace,
    Someday, somewhere!

AT WORST.

TO ——

Parceque nous avons le doute en nous.—V. H.

CHRISTMAS night, and tears of rain
Beating on my window pane,
Tears of rain as though in pity
On the dreary-lighted city:
Friend, and I have need of thee—
It is not as it used to be!

   Fainter now the younger years
Die along that mist of tears,
Darker lies the way before,
And the clouds are more and more;
I am standing here alone
Seeking help and finding none,
Crying out this Christmas night
Who will make my burden light?
Like a lost child in the rain
Crying loud, and all in vain,
For the old guide back again!

I have read my brother's face,
Earth is not a merry place;
Children laugh, but never after
Rings again our childhood's laughter;
Surely with increase of sorrow
Wisdom grows from morn to morrow,
And we burden life with pain
Hope may not unlearn again.

This was ever so, the best
Sought not pleasure, sought not rest;
Thinkest thou their lives were dear
Whom thou lovest to revere,
Bard, philosopher, and seer?
What was life to these who wrought
For a world that heeded not,
Wrought and taught and strove and fell
By the hands they loved too well!

This at least is stern and true,
They have shown thee what to do!
Follow thou, account it gain
Though thine happiness be pain!

Then there broke a little light
Down the dreariness of night :
Courage, courage, hast thou seen
Faith and doubt are near akin !
Were the future clear as day
None but fools could go astray,
None but fools could choose the gloom,
March in blindness into doom ;
Little merit were it then
To be worthy, to be men !

Only in a drifting sea
Still to struggle manfully,—
Little love where once we loved,
Changing hearts and friends disproved,
Though the olden hopes ring hollow,
Though ye dream effacement follow
On the brink where men despond
Seeing all so dim beyond,
Hoping little, asking less,
Full of human weariness,
Doubting—still to be as true
To the highest light we knew.

Still to choose the bitter rood,
Cling to what thy soul sees good,
Still to suffer and forbear
Doubting, this were worthy here

Then I knew a little star
Rose and glimmered, faint and far,
And a feeble light was cast
Up the shadows of the past.
Something surely time can save
From the silence of the grave,
Surely, though for days to come
Wail of prophecy be dumb,
Yet prophetic are those years
In the writing of their tears :
Something clearer now we know
Dark to wisdom long ago ;
Beauty lives and truth survives,
Harvested from fleeting lives,
More and more new day by day
Olden sorrows wane away,
Nothing sinks from good to worse
In the Ordered Universe.

AT WORST.

Brighter burns the little star,
Brighter light, but not less far;
Watch and watch and hold it fast,
Hope may turn to faith at last.

Therefore this is stern and true,
Well thou knowest what to do,
Labour on, and be thy fear
Not to read thy duty clear.
Wouldst thou rest upon the way,
Waste in sleep thy little day,
Murmur that the road is rough !
Time for sleep is long enough.
Up and do thy little best,
Soon thou canst not choose but rest !

Thou hast seen and thou must choose,
Only cowards dare refuse,
Choose, enough for thee to know,
Garnered from the long ago
Beauty lives, and Truth survives,
Harvest of unnumbered lives :

Therefore trebly fool to lie,
With thyself shall falsehood die!
Folly shall be dumb with thee
Down the dumb eternity!

Brighter beacons that sure Star
Where the hopes of ages are,
Plainer grows the upward road
Where the feet we follow trod!
Look what have they to oppose
In the stronghold of our foes!
We at least can suffer long
Whom that Star of Hope makes strong!
In the shadow dead and past
They shall all be lost at last.

Yet the wall must be assailed
Where 'tis hardest to be scaled,
Where the fight goes man for man
Plant thy foot-hold in the van!
Wide the fosses ridge to ridge,
Fallen bodies build a bridge,

AT WORST.

Stand or fall, heed not thy loss,
Surer feet shall win across!

Friend, how many storms together
You and I have yet to weather!
—We who once in clouded youth
Tried to find the Star of Truth—
Arm by arm and knee by knee
In the foremost of the free,
Till the fight of years be done,
And the Quiet Rest is won,
Till the new dawn gather fast,
Moonless night be overpast,
And the light break through at last.

1882.

AT BEST.

Nothing on earth like a noon of June !
In a quiet place with the heart in tune
Just to lie while the hours run
Watching and silent and drunk with sun !
Where you will so where flowers are,
And the noise of men and the whirl are far,
Just to listen and feel at rest
As here I lie on the earth's warm breast :
To look at the marvel of life that stirs
Where the meadow meets with the last great firs
At the dark wood's margin, and then to list
To the voice of Nature the optimist ;
While the birds and butterflies come and go,
And the best for them is the way they know,
And the grasses whisper, how well to be
On the meadows breast with the sun to see,
And the tree-arms wave and the lowliest one
Unenvied lifts for its share of sun.
And I heard of the brown bee, heather and thyme
Are more than the rose of the Paradise clime,

And the little larks, the mid-sky elves,
Said, how the poor world folk fret themselves,
While the mead in dew and the morning sky
Were made for singing, and so sing I.

Then wakes on a sudden the even-wind
From its noon-day drowse in the trees behind,
Whispering "hush," as it rustles through;
And the grasshoppers have a deal to do,
The beetle booms by the hedge-row way,
So busy at eve for his sleep all day,
The moth awakes, with "it's time for me,"
And drops like a down from the willow-tree,
The daisies close in the knee-deep hay,
And the sun-blind bats come out to play,
The twilight air has a scent of dew,
Shadows deepen and stars ensue.

This is the help when the love-springs dry
For the weary heart and the world-scared eye,
When the ranges narrow and hope is tired,
And the skies are dark for the vain-desired,

To turn again to the quiet way,
To pause and listen and learn to say,
We had sought amiss for the test of truth,
The joy is here and the ageless youth,
The cloud dispelled and the hope renewed,
The trust, the power, the certitude.

"WHETHER IN DAWN'S GREY GOLD."

Whether in dawn's grey gold, or in the noon
Serene, or under the red bars
Of sunset, or in nights of cloud-blown moon,
Or in the moonless company of stars;

Whether in winter with the jewelled snows,
Or in the lifting impulse of the spring,
Or when the summer's bridal beauty blows,
Or autumn reddens to the garnering,—

Oh, silent sequence of eternal laws!
O earth, and sun and moons and stars that range,
I trace the intent and the unknown cause
In all your voiceless eloquence of change:

How thou sufficest, nature, needest not
The strong man's effort or the weak man's wail,
The thing remembered or the thing forgot,
Secure and only impotent to fail!

O earth, in thee is anything out worn,
Has any loveliness endured to die?
One least good passed that shall not be reborn
To nobler use and more abundantly!

And wouldst thou put eternity to test,
Holding the witness of thy one day past !
Look down the aftertime and stand confessed
And wildered with the infinite at last !

Have we not sounded all philosophies
Up to the threshold of the door of death,
To acknowledge only that no knowledge is,
Nor aught to rest on if it be not faith ?

This is the end of knowledge, long desired,
That night will follow and day-dreams depart ;
Lay down thy longings—thou art very tired—
In calm submission on the great world's heart ;

Be trust thy triumph—having learned to mark
The straining upward and the growth of years,
The light returning alway through the dark,
The ample harvest of the ancient tears,

The Nothing falling to the earth in vain,
The sense that winds around us and above,
A promise breathing in the heart of pain
Conviction and supremacy of Love.

CREDO.

I will sing a song for the toilers, the song of the
   open ways,
The poem of human effort, the song of the works and
   days.

Come down by the crowded river,—do you think there
   are no songs here?
I will show you the song of songs, and the meaning of
   songs made clear;

In the tune of the hands that fashion, in the workers
   working aline,
The forge and the anvil smitten, and the marvel of
   long design:

Where the masts of the myriad ships reach far as the
   eye may scan,
And every stroke on the iron rings out the glory of
   man,

Tall pine of the snow-fed Norseland, oak strength of
    our island trees,
The might of the earth's surrender sent forth to fight
    with the seas :

Like a thought from the brain of a poet shall she fare
    with her sails unfurled
From the heart of the city of nations, the great pulse-
    beat of the world :

She shall lie becalmed on the waters in the glare of
    the sultry noons,
She shall glide through phosphor waves, as they read
    by the tropic moons :

And the mariner's boy shall wonder at the large
    unwonted stars,
The winged fish under her bow, and the strange birds
    lit on her spars.

O world not weary or old, fair world immortally new,
Speed fresh pioneers to battle with the infinite work
    to do !

CREDO.

Strike thou on the bolt exulting, young man with the knotted chest,
For the stroke of thine arm endures, and the worst gives way to the best!

Strike form and design and triumph from the old eternal strife,
Through the force controlled and mastered infuse the matter with life!

Now out on the craven adage, let it be with the ancient graves
The cry of the curse of labour, for that was the cry of slaves!

Let it speak to you this world's wonder, this conquering force and mind,
Oh, open your hearts, long-sleepers, and open your eyes, long blind!

Take heart, oh labouring strength, strike sure, oh masterly hands!
By the will informed on the conquered mass, the dream of the world expands;

All things grow possible now, thought's range has a
    wider scope,
The germ of faith in the things achieved is the seed of
    an infinite hope.

God's Now is a myriad years, and ye say that the end
    is long,
That the host will not be gathered, nor the hands of
    the few be strong;

A little while and a while we wait,—for the strength
    that the years beget,
To be bold for the strong conviction, have done with
    the half-regret,

To dare to confront and break through the old and
    the time-endeared,
To endure the imputed motive, and smile when the
    heart is seared.

For the price must be paid of purchase, and bitter it is
    to win,
It was lonelier once and darker, when of old they
    dared to begin;

But I know it must all come true, I have hope for the
  by-and-bye,
Or what were the wise men's wisdom, and why did
  the brave men die?

They carried a whole world's burden to a desolate
  grave for this;
How the lips that shall love hereafter will breathe
  their names in a kiss!

But the ways shall divide before us, the songs of all
  lands combine
In the loud victorious music that rings for the battle
  sign!

O child of the earth, who art thou, to sit in thy dumb
  despair?
Lo, thine old immortal mother is young for ever and
  fair,

With dower of all creations, enriched, she that cannot
  lose
Earth, generous, all-accepting, for whom doth the
  earth refuse?

All matter and hope and power, and range of a
　　thousand lands,
She hath given us unwithholding. Who is it hath
　　bound our hands?

We shall call them forth from the cities, away to the
　　fields of birth,
Not one shall be disherited, one hopeless in the
　　earth.

Oh, you that stand in the sunlight, unearned, could
　　you not forego
A share of your sun-warmed hill sweep for these in the
　　shade below?

You should be so glad to beckon, to call them up from
　　their night,
To watch for the form and order that is born in your
　　own fair light:

For never was aught lacked beauty, aught failed since
　　the world began,
In body or soul deformed to see, but the wrong was
　　done of man.

Have you fear for the chance of changes, is the bitter sweet of the past
The best that you dare to dream of, God's scheme for the world at last?

Do you think that there is no way but the worn unlovely road,
And there in the perfumed places are you casting about for God?

If you knew how safe is the truth, how little avail your Noes,
How the seed swells into the shoot, and how surely the young tree grows!

How truth is above your gauge, how it takes no count of the years,
How we smile at your half concessions, the doubt, the regrets, the fears!

For what have you strained to outstrip, hope winning of what in your strife?
Is there anything worth the winning in the antics you call life?

I am sad for you all, my brothers, to yourselves is the
    greater wrong,
You have seen but a part of the purpose, sung one bar
    out of the song.

Still somewhere hidden away, like the pearl on the
    ocean shelf,
With the drift and the sea's weed hiding, is the old
    god-imaged self ;

And I wish I could find some word that would ring on
    that soul's self true,
To pierce through the unessential to the pearl in the
    heart of you :

To strip you clean to the soul, of the mask, the seeming,
    the name,
And leave you naked and bare, to your beauty and in
    your shame.

Turn, turn from the forms and symbols, look into the
    heart instead,
There is more in the heart to guide than the words of
    the wisest head !

Where over all wandering mists, like a glory of light breaks through
On the love of the same things lovely, the sense of the same things true.

Therefore let us bar our hearts to never a man that lives,
For wider is love than life is, and I know that it grows as it gives.

Is there one that is self-absorbed dare look at the sky and sea?
Can hate dwell under the starlight, in the sun can a mean thing be?

Oh, all you great of the earth, come and read your lives in the graves!
On the lordly one and the lowly the tuft of the wild grass waves.

Do you see what has lived behind them, do you think when your days are sweet,
On these that have smoothed your highway with travel of weary feet?

Look, never one soft word spoken dies out on the
    quivering air,
But the load of the years is lightened, and the joy of
    it everywhere!

Here is love for you dead and nameless! Not in vain
    did one of you fall,
And the bond of the same wide being makes kinsmen
    out of us all:

There was count of them all before us, there was need
    of the lowliest ones,
I am child of you all, O fathers, and brother of you,
    O sons!

From you what the years inherit, the vast bewildering
    plan,
The light that is guide to effort, the hope and the
    help for man:

And strong by the strength you gave them the wise of
    the world are calm,
Where the riot and clamour of voices are lost in a
    louder psalm;

And shapes as of endless idols, this one with the hands
    red dyed,
The prince and the priest and the bigot, the saint with
    the bleeding side,

The chief and the crouching figures, the changeful
    murmur and cry,
The strain and urge of the moment, all this goes
    wildering by:

They are grown far-off and unreal, with the murmur
    of their complaint,
They are shadows at war with shadows, and the wail
    of them waxes faint;

Turn, turn from the cave's dark hollow! look up to
    the light and see,
Though thine eyes be dazed in the glory, the man that
    is yet to be!

Time's wings are at pause beside him, and calm is his
    heart's strong beat,
And the dust of these old dominions is flowerful round
    his feet.

Exult, we have won the midway, and the light has scared the gloom,
And we smile at the old sad sentence, we are freed from the endless doom.

Not heirs of a forfeit Godhead, degenerate, waning away,
But climbing, and all too slowly, from darkness into the day.

There is light in my eyes of dawning, of a fair world weary of sleep,
I see the new peopling islands, dominions over the deep,

Away to the ancient forests, and the wilds that are yet unwon,
Where the envious growth of creepers goes rivalling up to the sun;

Where the streams of the orient land roll out through their gates of gold,
Where the dizziest mountain summits were shrines of the faiths of old,

Where the well of the desert waters gives life to the
    lonely tree,
Where the tent of the turbaned nomad is set by the
    inland sea.

From the zone of the torrid summers to the uttermost
    ways of snow,
From the inland-men to the island-men shall the
    greeting of good-will go :

Peace, peace on the earth for ever, and we all forgotten
    so long,
But the air that they breathe is holy because of our
    sighs and song.

And their maids shall be pure as morning, their youth
    shall be taught no lie,
But the way shall be smooth and open for all men
    under the sky ;

They will build their new romances, new dreams of a
    world to be,
Conceive a sublimer out-come than the end of the
    world we see,

And the shadow shall pass we dwell in, till under the
    self-same sun
The names of the myriad nations are writ in the name
    of one;

What once in the dark strife ages the young Mace-
    donian planned,
When he flung his Bœotian chlamys by the sea on the
    Nile-mouth sand,

Saying, Here will I build me a city for all in their right
    of birth,
For my undivided nation, my people of all the
    earth.

He that had dared to reason with the wisest man of
    the wise,
And had looked to a grander vision with his young
    world-conquering eyes,

Who scorned at the Master's saying, of the born to be
    slave or free,
Seeing one same sun over all men, one wide earth
    girdling sea.

CREDO.

Rest, dead pioneers, rest well, bright spirits, and be content,
It is near on the day to march in, the night of the years is spent!

The arms of the dawn are reaching to gather the mist away,
And your star that the hill-peaks harboured grows dim in the rose of day.

I can see as it were in a vision the fulness of day unroll,
And the light of the sunrise cresting the hills with its aureole,

First red in the sky at dawning, wild cloud and the bode of storm,
But the winds are hushed and the clouds dispart for the feet of a queenly form.

On her brows is a crown of olive, her arms are outstretched afar,
She is robed in a rainbow's glory, and each of her eyes is a star.

The sword that she bears is broken, the arc of her wings is furled,
She is throned on the ancient mountains, and her smile goes over the world.

THE HERMIT'S TALE.

THE HERMIT'S TALE.

I, Prosper, from my hermit's solitude,
God's witness in this mountain,—I the least
Of all who seek salvation, as God knows,
Yet labouring somewhat for my fellows here
To his more glory, as a sinner may,
And trusting in the Merciful, Amen!
The hermit, Prosper, who am known to all
The dwellers in yon valleys, and what folk
Fare through these passes, pilgrims marching south,
And merchant trains and all who make for Rome,
Write down these words and lie not;—what befell
Here in this mountain, since the day He died,
The Merciful, eight hundred years and ten,
The eve of Easter as it drew to dawn,
To God's great glory;—what I know I tell.

Wild as its wont was winter in these crags,
Without this wall the snows were drifted high—

The wind's way through yon gully; but within,
Brave pine-logs blazed, for I have never lack,
So pilgrims pay their shelter, laying by
My winter store against the lonely days.
Weeks then and weeks had no soul fared this way;
The drifts lay round too deeply; and I thought,
How am I lonely in the hills with God
To keep my vigil on this Easter-eve!
But brief, ye know my life, sirs, and my vow.

It may be I had nodded at my beads,
But I was wide awake then,—see this page—
This is the copy that I made myself,
A winter's labour, written word for word,—
This page is doubled where I read that night
In John, in the twelfth chapter, where He saith,
" An any hear me and believe me not,
" I do not judge him,"—when the fire blazed high,
And as a sudden blast whirled by without,
The raw wind gusted in; thereat I turned,
And on yon threshold of the door beheld
The form of one so old and woe-begone,
So shrivelled, wrinkled, starved and shrunk and pale,

I shuddered back as one who stares at death ;—
So crossed myself, and as I moved his eyes
Piercing the shadow found the crucifix
Which stands to face for reverence entering ;—
There shot a scared look o'er his caverned brows,
A shiver rattled all his bony limbs,
And such a hollow whisper hissed, "Away!
"Thou art a holy man, away, away!
"Thou canst not shrive me, curse me from thy door!"
But while he struggled with the latch there broke
A clap like thunder, what I knew not then,
Only the door was barred without, and he
Fell down and cowered on the stony floor.

Dear God! a man, and all his throat and breast
Was bare and bitten by the searing wind,
The rime was frozen on his thin white hair,
And on such shreds of raiment as yet clung
To limbs so withered you had hardly deemed
Such fleshless skin could cling about the bone.
His hanks of beard were matted with the frost,
And icicled about his sunken lips,
Only the ghastly glitter of his eyes

Smote keen and quickly from the living soul,
And still he muttered as he shrank away,
" How long, Unmerciful! How long! Away!
" Thou canst not shrive me, and I may not die!"

   Then I, because I thought the man was faint
And weak with fasting, brought him bread and wine,
The wine they send me ever year by year,
For care of storm-lost brethren—set them by,
But he would none of it, he only groaned,
" The first who did not curse me!" shrinking back,
" The first who pitied, and he damns me worst."

   Then cried I, " Brother, whosoe'er thou art,
" Peace be upon thee in the Father's name,
" Peace in the Son's "——" Peace!" shrilled he back
      again,
" Blast not thy lips by bidding peace to me!
" Take back thy blessing, wait and hear my tale!'

" Hast heard of one shut out from death and hell,
" Damned to eternal wandering on earth,
" The stricken spirit of a living curse,
" The Jew, Ahasuerus? I am he!

"The last pollution of a leper race
"That feuded nations grow akin to hate!
"Hast heard of one that in the cross-way stood,
"And spat his mocking in the face of God?
"Curse me, and let me go, and no word more!
"He triumphed, I am judged,—say, God is good!"

Then, as I took his withered hand in mine,
And lifted up the fallen head, I saw
A shade of wonder seem to soften down
The fire of those indomitable eyes.

"The first who did not curse me! Dost thou deem
"I am some crazed unhappy wandering soul?
"What human life could live among these snows?
' But I, the accursed, in my living death
"Endure and suffer, live and wander on.—
"I walk the desert and the solitude
"Of mountain ranges, where no foot-tracks are;
"Oft have I flung me from the wall of rock
"And lighted scatheless, seeking death; I think,
"One gives the devil charge to bear me up:
"No sea will hide me, but I walk the waves;

"I am omnipotent except to die.
"By fields of slaughter and through plague-struck
         towns
"I pass, and look for ease in watching pain,
"And covet death that only takes not me.
"I have no count of years, I have outlived
"Men, empires, thoughts,—these pass, I heed them not,
"With my sole thought for ever I endure.
"Sleep has not ever closed these eyes of mine,
"I know no thirst nor hunger, only this,
"To be whirled on in impotence of pain
"From dawn to dark eternal, dark to dawn,
"Outside of pity and beyond remorse,
"A plague-spot and pollution, one to scare
"All innocent eyes,—I cannot look on joy,
"But I must blast it with a look of hate,
"And I have never heard one gentle word
"From child or woman, hounded on and on,
"The scapegoat of all mocking eyes on earth;
"The curse is on me by the doom of God."

Then, sirs, I rose, stung into speech at last,
And bade the devil, if such were in him,

Come forth and leave the human soul to peace,
And all the while he cowered on the ground.
"He does not curse me," muttered, and went on:
" Forbear thy pity, lest thou too be damned!
" Just God! Aye, very merciful and just!
" Were there no others mocking there but I?
" I had their silver, and I shouted loud
" With those who crucified: mercy and love
" They were not in our law,—and all you preach.
" We looked to find a prophet, and He came
" In humble raiment, with a crazy crew
" Of fisher-folk from Galilee!—Peace, peace, I know
" His triumph and my judgment by my doom.
" I had their money, and the Roman hound
" Had bowed to our tradition,—then it was
" His very Galileans turned and fled,—
" Peace, hear me through! I followed with the throng
" Howling and hooting. He was half dead then,
" Long hours of watching, left alone to die,
" Tortured the night through and condemned at
    dawn—
" The very stones were bleeding where He trod,
" And down His brows the black blood ran and dried,

"They pressed the thorns so deep into the flesh,
" He could not bear the heavy cross, He fell,—
" A King, we cried, will no one raise the King?
" A King, a Saviour, let Him raise Himself!
" And as He fell upon the bleeding stones,
" I laughed and mocked and spat in His white face!
" Away from me, away!—I saw His eyes,—
" The curse was on me as my mocking died.
" There struck a frozen horror to my heart,
" And, as I turned, I heard behind, beyond,
" The chorus of all angels in the height,
" Singing the triumph of the death of God."

"Nay, hear me yet,—I followed with the throng.
" These eyes that look into your eyes beheld
" Your cross reared high against the dark black heaven,
" A moment since so cloudless,—blue with spring,—
" I heard the words you cling to in your need
" Wafted across the still before the storm:
" I saw it all, the cry that came at last,
" ''Tis finished,'—there is naught you do not know:

" Then the earth reeled around us, and the wind
" Howled from the wilderness, then wailed the crowd,
" Turned, scattered, fled,— Jew, Roman, Gentile,
   Priest!
" And ever against the flashing skies the cross
" Stood fixed, enduring,—as there! there! And I
" My eyes were blinded—God, unmerciful!
" Were there no others mocked but I?—the hills
" Shook and the graves were rended, and the dust
" Darkened the whirlwind, as we fled, we fled.
" And ever and ever in these eyes of mine,
" In light in dark for ever burns that cross!
" Rings back my mocking on these ancient ears!
" And those, those eyes that curse me through the
   thorns!"

You know me, sirs, a man of simple mind,
Not very lettered, but a ready tongue,
To speak the word God whispers, His the praise!
I did not fail for reason then I think,
Not I, but that which through me answered back
The word of hope and faith and truth and life.

I cried, "The curse is only in thy heart,
" The living madness of a long remorse
" That drives thee on, as once the living hope
" Bore the divine in Patmos up through time,
" Until God took him ere the fire was quenched :
" He could not curse, He curse ! the Merciful ! "

I told him Hate and Love dwell not in one,
As fire and water mutually repel,
Vengeance and Mercy have an alien end,
If God be God, good must proceed of God !
Therefore, He could not curse, the Merciful.
And all this while he cowered at my feet,
Crept but a little nearer as I spoke,
" He *does* not curse me " muttered, and was still.

But something in me whispered, lo, the time,
The place of his redemption ! God is pleased
To work this wonder by thy hand : Arise,
Nerve all thy soul to effort, trust to God
To give the word thou needest now, Amen.

Then, sirs, I wrestled with that lonely soul,
I cannot tell my story word for word,

For some voice stronger than my voice spake then,—
And night went by and he lay at my feet,
And stared for ever on that crucifix,
Rocked to and fro, and moaned and murmured oft,
" He could not curse, not curse,—the Merciful ! "

"Sayst thou, He could not curse—but see this flesh,
" This driven wraith of life !—He could not curse.
" But is He not Almighty, and I live ? "

" Oh, half convinced against thy will," I cried,
" Yet steeled to bar the knocking hope away,
" If love were only frozen in thine heart,
" And hate the ice that binds its hidden spring,
" If this thy doom were mercy after all,
" Thy long atonement to redeem thy sin,
" If even now the smitten lips that breathed
" The word of mercy on the mocking crowd
" Were waiting, smiling, at the Gate of Heaven,
" If even now the wounded hands reached forth
" To take thine hand and guide the faltering feet,
" If love be love, and mercy be with God,

"Then wilt thou mock at love a second time,
" Be thine own curse for ever?"—Hark, he calls!

Then, as it were a mask of ice that thaws
When the rock-spring grows conscious of May sun,
His stony face grew softer, lips relaxed,—
I cried:

      " Uncurse thyself, and thou art free!
" This is the dark before the dawn, and I
" Stand here His witness, as of old Himself
" Spake on the mountain, ' Come ye unto Me
" ' All ye that labour.' Lo, He bids me now
" Lift thee and love thee, thee He died to help,
" Thou canst not choose but love Him! Rise and
      pray!"

Hereat it seemed as though a mist had dimmed
The fire that gleamed beneath his caverned brows,
And through the wrinkles of his thin sunk lips
There wreathed the ghostly semblance of a smile,
And once again, but very faintly now,
" He could not curse, the Merciful!"—he sighed,
Smiled outright now, and smiling so fell back

THE HERMIT'S TALE.

With stedfast eyes upon the crucifix,
And when I knelt to lift him he was dead,
While through the casement grew the Easter dawn.

    There, sirs, you have my story, word for word
I may not tell it,—for I spoke not then,
But something through me, greater than my voice.
I found with daybreak how a drift of snow
Blown up the lintel barred the door without.
What say you, sirs? It is an olden tale,
The wandering sinner's, and if God were pleased
To show the world such miracle of doom,
Such great atonement, and to work through me
The marvel of His mercy at the end,
Judge ye! I have my verdict, God's the praise!

    He lies there where on that red Easter dawn
I laid him, for the snows began to yield,
And all the spring months after fell no more;
The winds blew softly on the early year,
And in the growing days I hewed that cross
In the rock's surface to abide, and be
My witness to the world and his.
Ye have my story, what I know I tell.

PETRARCH:

A Monologue.

"Voi pur forse desidererete di sapere che homo io mi sia stato."—*Francesco Petrarca: Memorie del'a sua Vita.*

PETRARCH: A MONOLOGUE.

I.—PADUA.

Nay, friend Boccaccio, you do reason well,
The past were all forgotten,—let us leave
All rancorous harbourings to meaner men!
I said the change was sudden, for last year
I made long stay in Florence, in my land,
If lands of sires exiled be fatherland,
Yet found but frosty greeting though I came
With Padua's crown still green upon my brow,—
Disherited and orphaned of my own.

And now, you bring me greeting in the name
Of Florence, with such honeyed words as these,
With "Master, teacher, glory of our land!"
Such generous liberties, freewill to choose
My chair in your new made Academy,
Such terms of courtesy as never yet
So proud a township humbled to convey:
And I, how shall I answer? Had it been

Mine from the first so, in my father's land,
To wear this robe of honour, mine to watch
The Tuscan students gather to my chair,
To teach communion with the mighty dead,
The hero voices of the hero-time,
In the great Arno city, I had found
The end of all ambitions,—and you come
To bring me this from Florence ;—well, well, well.—
The change is somewhat sudden, I have said,
Yet am I not less grateful, who but we
Should be exempt from memories of wrong,
And gladly greet the late return of light
That lifts the shadows of things past and dead.

   Yet, friend Boccaccio, I would say, my years
Are measured, and by now the tide of days
Is set to its appointed ebb and flow :
My life has found new havens, and secure
From envious winds and storms that pass the bar.
And most of all my heart's desire is set
Toward my throne of exile, and a grave
Among the low French cypresses ; the years
Grow more and many since I sojourned there,

Where all my days of youth were glorified,
Where most of all my name is linked with earth.

   Friend, say in Florence that I thank them well,
And take their late repentance to my heart,
As pledge of labours that were not in vain,
And crown of all my honours, but my years
Are many, and now I go a pilgrimage
To rest awhile by a belovéd grave,
And commune with a presence I shall find
About the the haunted meadows of Vaucluse.

II.—AVIGNON.

Still winds the Rhone between the level fields,
And all so changed yet changeless,—the white rocks
Far off the towers of Avignon, and last
The line of broken hill; these many days
I wandered in a dream, until last night
I seemed to stand on some great mountain ridge
High in the twilight glimmering to dawn,
With the mist rolling under and the chasm,
Blue depths unfathomable, and overhead
Pale stars and silence and the infinite.
Then seemed one star to waft down from its place,
Taking a form that floated in the dawn,—
The vision waited for that was to come.
But in her eyes was that eternal calm
Of those that gaze on angels, and her hair
Was rays of moonlight wandering on her brow,
And all so pale and ghostly,—and I stood

Over the slumbering earth, there was no sound,
Only she pointed upwards, and I knew
The sense of something speaking in my soul
Telling of joys transcending human thought,
Foretasting the eternity of Love.
Then right into the dawn she passed and left
The burning of her kiss upon my brow.

Then all the day grew round me where I stood.
And far across the sundering vales it broke
On peaks of morning very near the sky,
Still dark between us lay the sundering deep
With twilight heavy on the town of towers,
The sleeping and the watchers in the world.
And then it seemed from yonder hills her voice
Mixed with innumerable harmonies
Wafted toward me on the wave of dawn,
Leading a quire of voices in the height
That died in music with the waning star,
Saying, "go down, though it be twilight yet.
" For where is life is ever need of love,
" Go down and work a little while, and wait.
" The suns are measured and the days are told,

" But time is shoreless, after life is life,
" And after travail rest, and surely light
" Better than sun and moon and all the stars,
" And finding after seeking, and for love
" One home to which the many ways converge."

III.—ARQUA.

I am an old man now, my life has been
Endowed beyond my fellows—honours, fame,
And good report in store above my due.
And I have written many books; explored
The ancient wisdom of the mighty dead,
Through me regenerate; philosopher,
Poet, and scholar, pattern to the youth
In all the schools from Avignon to Rome;
The friend of Popes and Princes—styled, in short,
Boccaccio says, the "glory of our age";
He brought that word from Florence—from my land!
Therefore, as one who laboured not in vain,
Have I bequeathed my riches to the world.
There lie my songs, themes, epics—one word more,
Here at the last, when I record my gain,
The best, the harvest, and the truth I found,
The soul of my philosophy remains
Love only: first, the one, the spiritual love,
That is the loadstar and the light of life,
And the hereafter haply—as I deem,

Since love at highest needs no earthly hope :
And then that other love inspired of this,
The all-embracing, all-forgiving love ;
The love that labours for the rest, endures,
And gives the world its earnest, that is all
Doubt has no part in, when we stand for truth,
And every heart is great enough for love,
As every soul is for eternity.

Now I will tell my story in few words.
In life's young spring there met me on my way
A spirit fashioned in no mortal mould,
But one whose earthly sojourn seemed to me
A revelation of the holier life,
A benediction from the home of heaven.
It was at morning song on the sixth day
Of the fourth month, the spring of year and youth.
In Santa Chiara's church, at Avignon,
I saw my lady of the blessed name,
And on the pulseless current of my thought
There flashed the change, the glory, and the doom.
And that same hour, the hour of morning song,
The same sixth day of that same April tide,

Twice ten years after, was she taken hence.
Her stainless body on the day she died
They laid to rest in its appointed place,
And her pure spirit I am bold to say
Went back to God, by whose good gift it came;
But I misfortuned then to be from home
And in Verona, knowing not my loss.

Now here make I my record, in my love
For Laura was no one base thought, nor vile;
I think not anything a man might blame,
Unless it were that love's excess; this much
Let no man doubt, whate'er my life hath been,
All that I am that by her grace am I,
Nor have I looked for other praise than hers
Who drew my spirit to her own pure light,
And stayed my gaze upon abiding things;
And there was never one I cared to please
Save her alone, whose fair ensample stands
Like the saint's lily in a stormy world,
Changeless and sweet and loveable and white,
Whom envy found no fault in to assail,
And faith assigns the circle of the saints.

Therefore, I say, love only; life shall prove
The need of loving. Many a man sees truth,
Knows the sheer way he half would choose to climb,
But little needs and fleeting aims withhold
The still strong step should mount to meet the
    dawn.
To see the truth is somewhat,—just to guage
The reach and effort, but to be the man
One would have men be, seek no meaner gains
But make the ideal real—this to do
She shewed me, having that great love for hope,
Through chance and change to glorify the end.
Who loves not pity, for none loves in vain,
Though here on earth it must suffice to know
Love is the lover's first, and the beloved's
In less degree, so incomplete at best.
But after, he who saw life's end in love,
Shall he not find the need he recognized
In some divine, unfathomable way
Returning and enfolding him at last?
I have my hope, I reason not with faith.—
If love be life's end, then the end of love
Remains, is surely to be loved again.

ARQUA.

My best on earth was out of reach for me,
Past striving for and only all life long
A far-off benediction and a hope:
But this I know, so much of mine was hers,
Clasped close, so close, no other life shall mark
Its seal on hers to hold our souls apart
When soul meets soul with nothing more between,
Till then I tarry and abide my doom.

Therefore, I would that in far years to be,
When great things grow forgotten, tides of change,
Events of import shadow-like and dim,
If aught that sounds on many tongues to-day
Of all I strove to make abiding here,
Should find a corner in men's hearts and breathe
Among hereafter voices, they should tell
Not of my epic that they crowned me for,
Not of the kinship with the hero-time,
But how once lived a lover in the world
Who prized the myrtle better than the bay,
Who sang one master-song to many keys,
Whose faith this was, and, loving once and well,
He gave his lady all a poet may,
The glory of an everlasting name.

THE END OF THE QUARREL.

Twas to-night we should have met,
    For our quarrel might not mend,
Each to answer for his hate
    To the bitter end.

And to-day on either hand—
    Hollow-hearted as despair,—
By a bed of death we stand,
    And are answered there.

Both have lost and neither won,
    Here before that tranquil brow
Passion and desire are done,
    All ended now.

On her maiden bed she lay,
    Very beautiful and calm,
While without the Frati pray,—
    Sing a dreary psalm.

THE END OF THE QUARREL.

Mine or thine the heavier loss,
    Pillowed on that bier of flowers!
On her bosom lies the cross—
    And the knives in ours!

But the fierce eyes flash no more,
    And the bitter lips are dumb,
We two met there as before,—
    Death had overcome.

And I looked into his eyes,
    And I looked upon her rest,
Calmly now I dared surmise
    She had loved him best.

Then he reaches forth his hand—
    Be it spoken to his praise—
Needs no word to understand,
    And we go our ways.

JUBA'S DEATH.

Cæsar landing and Pompey dead;
Sittius beaten and Juba fled!

Lines that close in a narrow ring,
And the gates of Zama shut on the king!

Swift as flight to the end of day,
The king and the Roman ride away.

Numidian Juba, the Roman's friend,
Friendless, crownless, and near the end,

With old Petreius scored with scars,
Won for Rome in the Spanish wars;

A kingdom lost and an empire won—
And over the desert sinks the sun!

Into a village the old men ride
As the hours draw to the eventide,

And the swarthy landfolk quake to see
The blood splashed over their horses' knee.

" Scour the village in haste and bring
" What cheer ye have, it is I, the king ! "

Side by side in the village street
The king and the Roman sat at meat.

The sun stood still on the desert line
As they filled their helms to the brim with wine,

And first they poured with their bloody hands
A helmet full in the thirsty sands.

" In many a battle side by side,
" Comrade mine, were we used to ride."

" To the god of battles," the red king saith,
" To the good friends gone, and the truce of death !

" Fill me again, and then drink deep,
" Night draws on and it's time to sleep."

A star dawned clear in the blue o'erhead
As the red king bared his sword and said,

"Comrade mine, by the love you bear,
"Draw your blade from its sheath and swear,

"If first I fall in the loyal strife
"We will do for death as of old for life.

"Grip me the hand and swear as I
"On the self same sword you will fall and die!"

Face to face by the desert sand
The king and the Roman take their stand.

"Now, old friend, for the true sword-play,
"Face to face in the warrior way!"

And the large stars grew in the Eastern sky;
Merry was life and—now to die!

Flashed their blades in the starry light,
Clashed the steel on the still of night,

Laughed they hoarse as the blows fell fast;
Merry his laugh who laughs at last.

Parry and counter and—"curse the sand!"
Thurst and parry and—"hold thine hand!"

A fall! no groan, but a clutch at dust—
The king struck home with a master thrust!

Forcing the blade out, jagged and gored,
Fell himself on the self same sword.

So they lay in the starlight side by side—
That was the way that the red king died!

A PICTURE.

Hedge-rows withered and sere,
   Hardly a leaf on the trees,
Waifs of the waning year
   Tossed on a fitful breeze!

Peasant-folk gathering in
   The last that the damp earth yields,
Only the rooks to glean
   Over the tired fields!

Low cloud-lines hurrying west
   Heavy with rain and grey,
Over the brown hill-crest,—
   All things passing away.

A DEDICATION.

If I could have painted pictures
   I would like to have set you there,
In a robe of the hue of amber,
   With a star's light in your hair ;
With fondling hands that rested
   On the head of a little child ;
Eyes ocean deep with kindness
   And lips that sighing smiled,
   That the children of the city
     Might come to my shrine and say,
   Look, that is the angel, Pity,
     Will hearken when we pray.

I surely had used my virtue
   In the work that you desired,
And made the joy eternal
   Which the thought of you inspired.
But I may not paint you in pictures,
   Not make the marble live,

Nor match your voice with music;
And all that I have to give
Are these poor songs I treasure
Since I the singer knew,
They shadowed in their measure
The light I loved in you.

By the Same Author.

POEMS IN MANY LANDS.

Second Edition, Crown 8vo, cloth, gilt tops, price 5s.

"Mr. Rodd's special qualities are command of agreeable sounds, pathos, simplicity, and sentiment."—*Saturday Review.*

"There is an unmistakable ring in the verse. It may or may not be developed into a real powerful music, the music that is full of thought, as well as of sound. Meanwhile it is there, and is quite sufficient to raise this volume considerably above the average of contemporary verse." —*Spectator.*

"Few more enjoyable volumes of verse have made their appearance of late than Mr. R. Rodd's *Poems in Many Lands.*"—*Scotsman.*

"It is hardly rash to say that of the younger poets none exhibit a truer love of nature, or a more intimate knowledge of her phenomena."—*Academy.*

"We have quoted at unusual length from Mr. Rodd's collection, because, aside from the clear promise of better things to come, the positive excellence of his workmanship seemed to challenge for him a wide audience." —*The Sun, New York.*

DAVID STOTT, 370, OXFORD STREET, LONDON, W.

www.ingramcontent.com/pod-product-compliance
Lightning Source LLC
Chambersburg PA
CBHW031813230426
43669CB00009B/1119